Enlightening Tales

Enlightening Tales

As Told By
Sri Swami Satchidananda

Edited by Swami Karunananda
Illustrated by Uma Schreiber
With a Foreword by Carole King

Integral Yoga® Publications
Satchidananda Ashram–Yogaville
Buckingham, Virginia

Library of Congress Cataloging-in-Publication Data

Satchidananda, Swami.
     Enlightening Tales as told by Sri Swami Satchidananda/edited by Swami Karunananda;
illustrated by Uma Schreiber; with a foreword by Carole King.
     p.   cm.
     ISBN 0-932040-48-9
     1. Religious life—Hinduism.   I. Karunananda, Swami
BL 1237.34.S27   1996   96-15582
294.5'43—dc20   CIP

Books by Sri Swami Satchidananda

Integral Yoga Hatha
Integral Yoga: The Yoga Sutras of Patanjali
The Living Gita: The Complete Bhagavad Gita
The Golden Present (Daily Readings)
Beyond Words
To Know Your Self
Kailash Journal
Guru and Disciple
The Healthy Vegetarian
Integral Yoga Meditation booklet
  (with audio cassette instruction)
Integral Yoga Hatha booklet
  (with audio cassette instruction)

Books about Sri Swami Satchidananda

Sri Swami Satchidananda: Apostle of Peace
The Master's Touch

Other Books from Integral Yoga® Publications

Imagine That: A Child's Guide to Yoga
LOTUS Prayer Book
Dictionary of Sanskrit Names
Yoga for Kids—by Kids

For all who wonder and seek
and love a good story—
May you find the Source of all wonder
and be filled with Love and Light.

Acknowledgements

Integral Yoga® Publications is happy to present this volume of forty-seven

Enlightening Tales as told by Sri Swami Satchidananda

in honor of the forty-seventh anniversary of Sri Swamiji's initiation

into the Holy Order of Sannyas.

The publication of this book was made possible through the dedicated service and heartfelt support of the following people:

Swami Sharadananda and Kumari de Sachy, Ed.D. for editorial assistance;

Uma Schreiber for the beautiful illustrations;

Hari Barker of Integral Yoga® Publications for overseeing the book's production;

Ganesh MacIsaac for his guidance concerning design and production;

Gurudas Natarajan for helping to prepare the manuscript for publication;

Swami Sarvaananda for helping to facilitate the final preparation of the manuscript;

Palace Press International for the layout and design, including the illuminated letters at the beginning of each story;

Abhaya Thiele for typing assistance;

Sister Ramani and Swami Gangeshwarananda for proofreading;

Swami Hamsananda for transcribing and indexing Sri Swamiji's talks; and all the dedicated souls who have recorded and preserved these teachings over the years.

We thank them all for their noble and loving service. May God bless them with all health, happiness, peace, and prosperity.

Foreword

Sri Swami Satchidananda arrived in America at a time when people were just beginning to look for more spiritual awareness than Western society seemed to offer. In 1969, the year of the original Woodstock, I was looking for a method of physical exercise. I could have taken a dance class, but instead found a Hatha Yoga class offered at the Integral Yoga Institute. In time, I became a Hatha Yoga teacher and began exploring other branches of Yoga at the Institute, and in doing so, began a long-time friendship with Sri Swami Satchidananda.

"Swamiji," as I've always thought of him, is a genuinely gifted teacher. He teaches by example, practicing what he teaches. I remember the first *satsangs* I attended that he conducted. The quiet presence of this tall man with long hair and a flowing beard, dressed in orange, drew us all closer together. During our discussion periods, his answers to complicated questions were so simple as to make one ask, "Why didn't I know that?" His answer was, "You did."

The simplicity of Swamiji's philosophy, based on the science of Yoga, continues to enlighten millions the world over. Becoming an octogenarian doesn't seem to have slowed him down. This collection of Swamiji's *Enlightening Tales* was put together for children, including those of us who reside in grown-up bodies. If you are not seeking enlightenment, don't worry—the stories will entertain you, and my guess is that enlightenment will find you anyway. The stories are derived from India's cultural heritage, but each has a lesson which holds true universally whatever your religious or cultural background. May you find peace, enjoyment, and comfort within.

—Carole King

Editor's Preface

Once upon a time, in a faraway land across the sea, there lived a most unusual man. He seemed quite normal at first—and no one suspected the great adventures and challenges that awaited him. For though he seemed rather ordinary on the outside, inside he had a most extraordinary idea.

He had heard of a mysterious, hidden kingdom that contained the greatest treasures, beyond anything anyone could ever imagine. He had also heard that anyone who went to the kingdom experienced so much happiness and joy that they were never the same again. He decided to find that place at any cost, and his quest began. As the years rolled by, he was to slay many demons, conquer the greatest foes, and one glorious day, discover that transcendental realm of peace and bliss.

It was so wonderful; it surpassed anything he had ever heard about it. The man thought, "Everyone should know about this place. It is so fantastic. I wish everyone could experience the peace and joy that I am feeling."

When he returned home, everyone experienced a great change in him. He was always happy. Nothing that happened ever saddened or frightened him. He never worried about anything and just seemed to surf over all the waves in life that overwhelmed everyone else. And he seemed to have a special golden glow and a twinkle in his eye that were just so delightful.

So people began to seek him out—mostly because they just felt good being with him. Somehow, their burdens felt lighter in his presence, and what had seemed like insurmountable problems were easily resolved. Word spread about him, and more and more people came.

One day, a traveler came to see the man and told him of a distant land of great prosperity and promise that was falling into chaos and confusion. Many of the inhabitants there, especially the younger ones, were desperately seeking a way out of all the turmoil and despair.

The traveler said to the man, "You should go there; I'll arrange everything."

And that is how, on July 31, 1966, His Holiness Sri Swami Satchidananda arrived in New York City. He left the idyllic, natural paradise of Ceylon (now Sri Lanka) and found himself in the Big Apple, which was crowded, noisy, and most unnatural. "What am I doing here?" he wondered. But he didn't have long to ponder, for, immediately, he was surrounded by those very young men and women the traveler had told him about. Just as the traveler had described, these young people were adrift in a sea of confusion and delusion, but the man could see that their longing for freedom and happiness was strong, and that their hearts were pure. He was totally captivated by their sincerity and determination.

So, he began to teach them about the extraordinary kingdom with all its treasures and how they, too, could find it—for it existed within their very own hearts. And very often, he told them stories about the kingdom: about other noble and courageous souls who had journeyed there, about the trials and tribulations along the way, and about the great fun they would have when they got there. There were also stories about how to make their day-to-day lives more fun, how with the proper attitude and approach, every moment of every day could be another step toward that grand discovery.

It has been the greatest blessing during the past three decades to have heard these enlightening tales from my beloved Master and to have learned about the possibilities for growth, transformation and, ultimately, freedom from all suffering.

I remember the first time I saw Sri Gurudev. I had recently graduated from college and was filled with a sense of emptiness and a deep longing for peace. His eyes met mine and, in that instant, I knew that he had found everything I was seeking. It was so incredible to be in his presence, to see a great Light in the midst of the darkness and to know that there was hope, that the peace I sought could be attained; because here was someone standing before me who totally embodied that peace. Then and there, I knew that the rest of my life would be spent following his teachings so that I could experience that peace and joy myself.

It is with the greatest joy that we present these teachings in this volume of *Enlightening Tales as told by Sri Swami Satchidananda*. It is our hope

Editor's Preface

that the stories will delight and uplift one and all. A devotee of Sri Gurudev once remarked, "They are stories that can help put children to sleep and wake up their parents." They are simple enough for a youngster to understand and profound enough to stir the consciousness of the most earnest spiritual aspirant.

The stories are accompanied by illustrations created in the Indian style especially for this book. We are very grateful to Uma Schreiber for these beautiful, pictorial renderings of the teachings. Not only do they delight the eyes, but they also help to impress the message of the stories deep in the heart.

To assist the reader, we have also included a glossary of Sanskrit terms at the end of the book. Very often, when a Sanskrit word is used in a story, it is directly followed by its meaning in parentheses.

Now, it's time to settle into a comfortable chair in a cozy corner somewhere. If there are children or friends nearby, gather them 'round—because everyone loves a good story. Are you ready? Adventure, surprises, and true wisdom await you. . .

—Swami Karunananda
Satchidananda Ashram–Yogaville
June 1996

Introduction
by Sri Swami Satchidananda

If you really want to learn, you will find that the entire nature is a book of knowledge. It can teach you everything you need to know. All the knowledge that you seek is freely available in this universe-ity. You don't have to go to a library; even the tiniest little thing can teach you a big lesson. The great teachers understood this; that is why they used examples from ordinary life to convey important truths. This can be seen in the beautiful stories and parables they told to their students.

That is how they taught—with very simple examples to bring out great truths. Many of the great sages and saints were just simple people. They seldom quoted from scriptures, because they didn't even read. They lived with nature, and what they, themselves, were learning directly from nature, they brought out in the form of stories. Then, when the people saw the ordinary, natural things in their daily lives, they were reminded of the highest truths.

Another reason that most of the great teachers taught in the form of stories is that people often forget the plain truth, because it's just plain. But they can easily remember a story. And by remembering the story, they can remember the teaching, also.

So the great teachers often presented the higher truths through stories—and the stories are very simple. In fact, the truth itself is very simple. Sometimes, our complicated minds don't want to accept that. They question, "Could it really be that simple?" A complicated mind doesn't want to accept simple things.

That is why the kingdom—real peace and joy—lies among the children. As the great sage Sri Ramakrishna Paramahamsa would often say, "Forget everything that you have learned. Become like a child again, and you will experience God right now."

These stories are for children of all ages. They contain within them the ancient wisdom and universal teachings of the great sages and saints of India, and are golden keys for true success in life. May you apply them well and experience all health, happiness, peace, and prosperity.

Contents

Dedication   7
Acknowledgements   8
Foreword   9
Preface   11
Introduction   15
List of Illustrations   19

Stories

The Key to Enlightenment   21
It's All for Good   25
Never Give Up!   29
The Sculptor and His Son   30
A Drop of Honey   33
Two Stones   36
The Swami and the Cow   38
A Perfect Lie   41
How to Build a Temple   42
The Apple Tree   44
As You Think, So You Become   45
The Beggar King   48
The Butcher and the Yogi   51
The Saint and the Scorpion   54
The Man Who Overcame Anger   56
The Wedding Guest   57
The Imitation Saint   58
The Golden Mongoose   62
The Demon Who Was Turned to Ash   64
The Milkmaid   66

The Boy Who Made God Eat His Pudding   69
You Are What You Eat   72
How to Stop an Elephant   74
The Greedy Milkman   77
You Can Have It All   78
The Conference on Light   79
Two Boatmen   81
A Stone for God   83
The Fox and the Lice   85
The Lion and the Sheep   86
The Demon and the Curly Hair   88
The Power of Maya   91
True Surrender   94
The Puzzle   97
The World Is Your Projection   99
God or Dog?   100
When Will You See God?   103
King Janaka's Enlightenment   104
Who Am I?   109
Let the Sun Shine In   111
The Poor Man's Karma   112
The Pilgrimage   115
The Horoscope   117
Bringing a Donkey to Market   118
The Secret of Happiness   121
The Man Who Did Nothing   123
The Last Straw   125

Glossary   127

Illustrations

1. It's All for Good   27
2. A Drop of Honey   35
3. A Perfect Lie   40
4. As You Think, So You Become   46
5. The Saint and the Scorpion   55
6. The Imitation Saint   60
7. The Milkmaid   67
8. How to Stop an Elephant   75
9. Two Boatmen   82
10. The Demon and the Curly Hair   89
11. True Surrender   95
12. God or Dog?   101
13. King Janaka's Enlightenment   106
14. The Poor Man's Karma   113
15. Bringing a Donkey to Market   119

The Key to Enlightenment

A man once went to an ashram seeking enlightenment. He bowed down before the swami and said, "I'm interested in knowing the Self. I want to find peace. Please give me this wisdom."

The swami smiled at him and said, "Poor man, you are going to die in ten days. It's too late."

The man was shocked. "You mean that I'm really going to die in ten days?"

"Yes, I see Death coming to you. It's very close."

"What am I to do, Swami? Is there anything you can teach me?"

"It's not that easy. Many people practice for years and still don't find wisdom."

But the man kept insisting, so the swami finally said, "Okay. Occasionally, I might make a mistake. Go home, and if by chance you live longer than ten days, come back to me. Then I will teach you."

The man returned home with a heavy heart. Some friends came to see him and asked, "Why are you looking so sad?"

"Well, the swami at the ashram said that I would die within ten days. I really don't know what to do. I have committed many sins, and I don't know how to atone for them."

At that moment, the man's accountant came and said, "Sir, we have to sue that man who owes you money."

But the man answered: "Forget about it. I loaned him money because I have more than enough. If I didn't have enough for my own expenses, I wouldn't have given him the loan. If he can't pay it back now, what's the use of sending him to jail? If he pays, all right. Otherwise, tell him that I am canceling the debt. He can enjoy the money." The accountant was very surprised, because the previous day the man had told him to confront the borrower and demand full payment plus compound interest.

Then the man called his brother, whom he had not seen in ten years, and asked him to come visit him. The brother was very surprised, because the man once told him that he would always consider him a deadly enemy. After much hesitation, the brother finally said, "All right, I'll come see you tomorrow."

The next day, the man who was going to die was seated by the window, watching for his brother. As soon as he saw his brother, he rushed to meet him. He embraced him and said, "My dear brother, please forgive me. I have misunderstood you all these years. Let's forget our enmity and become brothers and friends again." Then, one after another, he started calling his enemies and making friends with them all.

The next day, he called the accountant to find out how much money he had in the bank. It was really a lot. So he put aside some for his children's education, and with all the rest, he wrote checks to different institutions and worthy groups, which began using the money to help the sick and feed the poor.

Everyone began to wonder, "What's happening to him? All of a sudden, he's really becoming a generous, broad-minded man. He's making friends with everyone and giving everything to charity." They didn't know that he was supposed to die within a few days.

Finally, there were just two days left. He hadn't been able to eat for worry, and he had become very weak. He now had to stay in bed. He'd learned some Yoga and didn't discriminate among religions, so he invited a Catholic monk to come and read the Bible, a Hindu monk to recite the *Bhagavad Gita,* and some yogis to chant. His idea was to hear as many nice prayers as possible before he died.

By now, the whole town had come to know of him, and everybody was praising him. His name was in all the headlines. The tenth day came, and he told everyone, "I've finished my work. Don't bother me anymore. I'm going to sit down and meditate." He started repeating a mantra and waited for Death to come.

He looked at his watch. It was midnight of the tenth day. Something was wrong. The swami had said ten days. He asked his servants to go recheck all the doors. He had instructed them to leave all the doors unlocked so that Death could easily enter.

Now, even though he felt weak, he called some friends and asked them, "Please, take me to the swami." By that time, there were hundreds of people willing to do anything he asked. So they all went to the ashram, and when they arrived, the man fell down at the swami's feet, saying, "Swami, what has happened to your prediction? I didn't die."

"Yes, I see that you didn't die. Something must have gone wrong somewhere. The Lord of Death was probably just delayed. Wait here for another day and see if he comes. If he doesn't come, I will teach you."

So, the man sat in a room and meditated. The eleventh day also passed. He got up and said, "Swami, I'm still alive. Death hasn't come. At least now, please teach me true wisdom."

The swami smiled at him and said, "But, I've already taught you."

"What?" said the man. "I don't understand. You didn't teach me anything!"

"Well, what have you been doing for the last ten days? How many lies did you tell? How many enemies did you make? How much black market business did you do?"

"Swami, how could I do any of those things? I made up with all my enemies and gave everything to charity. I became a very good man because there was no time to waste. I knew I was going to die, and I didn't want to die with a bad name, so I patched up everything."

"What did others think of you before?"

"Nobody liked me. They said I was good-for-nothing, that I was a very bad man."

"And now, what do they say?"

"When I leave the house, everybody praises me, and there are many articles in the paper about me. They all seem to like me. They call me a great, saintly man."

"Are you happy about it?"

"Oh, yes, swami. Absolutely! I'm happy when everybody likes me, and I like everybody."

"Good. Then go back home. Know that you may die any minute, and don't make anyone your enemy. Live the same way that you have been living these past ten days. That is the essence of Yoga. Then you will always know peace. That is wisdom."

Enlightening Tales

Does anyone know when he or she is going to die? No. It can happen any minute. So why create enemies? Why tell lies? Live the Golden Rule as best you can. Let your entire life be a sacrifice for humanity. That is the goal of Yoga; that is the highest wisdom.

It's All for Good

nce upon a time, there was a king who had a wonderful, wise minister. The minister was very loyal and devoted to his sovereign, and the king would never leave the palace without the minister at his side. They were always together.

One day, as the king was cutting a piece of fruit, he accidentally cut his finger. While it was being treated, he asked the minister why this had happened. "I was being so careful," he explained, "but the knife just seemed to slip all by itself and gave me this deep cut."

The minister simply smiled at him and said, "Don't worry, Your Majesty; it's all for good."

The king became furious. "What kind of answer is that? I cut my finger! The blood is pouring out, and it hurts so much. Yet, you stand there and calmly say, 'It's all for good.' If that's all you care for me, I don't want you around anymore!"

The king called for his guards and told them to throw the minister in jail. As he was being taken away, the minister simply said, "As you wish, Your Majesty. No doubt, this, also, is for good." And he quietly submitted to the imprisonment.

Several days later, the king decided to go hunting. He went far into the forest with a large group of companions. At one point, he started chasing a beautiful deer. Since his horse was the fastest one, he was soon way ahead of the rest of the party. Still, the deer managed to escape. Before he knew it, the king had gone very deep into the jungle and was lost.

Fortunately, the king had been on many adventures, and he stayed calm. But he was very tired and thirsty. Nearby, there was a big green tree with a small brook running past it. He drank his fill, then leaned against the tree, and fell asleep in the shade.

After a while, he was awakened by a rustling sound. He slowly opened his eyes, and what he saw made him freeze. A huge lion was standing right next to him, and it was sniffing his body! The king didn't know what to do, so he just sat still, watching the lion. The lion continued to sniff him all over. Then, suddenly, as it was sniffing one of the king's hands, it drew back, snorted, and ran away.

The king was amazed at his good fortune! Of course, he had been so frightened that there was plenty of adrenaline pumping; he was wide awake now! He leaped up and began shouting for his hunting companions, and, eventually, they found him. "Listen," he told them, "a lion came while I was sleeping. It was huge and ferocious-looking. It was all ready to eat me, but something mysterious happened. All of a sudden, it just ran off!"

"That's wonderful!" they exclaimed. "What luck!" But none of them could explain what had happened. Then the king remembered his wise minister, who had always been able to explain such things.

When they returned to the palace, he had the minister brought from jail. He told him the whole story, to the last detail.

The minister simply said, "It's all for good, Your Majesty."

"What do you mean 'all for good'? That doesn't explain why the lion just went away without even biting me. What is the reason for this?"

"Your Majesty, the lion is the king of beasts, just as you are the king of people. When somebody offers you a fruit, it should be a clean and unblemished one. The lion wants his food that way, too. When it came and looked at you and sniffed you, it could tell there was something wrong. The minute it smelled the cut finger, it knew that you were not fit for the king of beasts. So you see, Sire, the cut finger saved your life. Now do you understand that it's all for good?"

"You're absolutely right," the king replied. "As soon as the lion sniffed my hand, it snorted as if in disgust. Then it ran off. You knew what you were saying all along. I'm so sorry that I had you locked up. But tell me something: as they took you off to jail, you said, 'This, also, is for good.' What is the good that happened by your imprisonment?"

"Your Majesty," the minister replied, "you know that, ordinarily, we are never separated. Surely, I would have been with you on the hunt and would have raced after you through the jungle. Then we would have both been sleeping under the tree when the lion arrived. He would still have rejected you, but he would probably have swallowed me because I had no

cuts. Because you put me in jail, my life was saved. So, you see, it's all for good."

Adversities are blessings in disguise. You may not be able to see the benefit until much later, but it is there. Have faith in the positive outcome.

Never Give Up!

 n olden times, there was a king of Scotland named Robert Bruce. He fought with his enemy six times, and each time he was defeated in battle. He lost everything: his kingdom, his wealth, all that he had. He lost all hope, ran away, and hid himself in a cave. He felt that he didn't even want to live anymore.

King Robert was planning to commit suicide when he noticed a spider trying to build a web. To build the web, the spider first had to put the central thread from the ground to the roof. The spider jumped, missed the roof, and fell down. Again it jumped, fell short, and came down. Six times, the spider jumped and fell down. King Robert was counting. The seventh time, the spider jumped and at last reached its goal.

"Well," thought King Robert, "if a little spider can have that kind of hope and tenacity, and ultimately succeed, why can't I? I'm not going to commit suicide. I'm going to fight again, and this time I'm going to win, just like the spider!" And he went out, gathered his troops, and won the war.

Never, never give up! Don't even allow the word "impossible" to be a part of your vocabulary. Everything is possible. That should be our attitude in life.

The Sculptor and His Son

here was once a great sculptor who was very well-known—the top-most sculptor of his age. He also served as the royal sculptor and was highly praised by the king. The sculptor's son wished to follow in his father's footsteps and even to excel his father. So the son worked very hard, and every time he did something beautiful, he invited his father to see it. The father would come and say, "It's all right, but it could be better." Then the son would go back and work on another sculpture, and this one would be much better. Again the father would come and say, "It's better than the previous one, but it still could be better." This happened many, many times.

Gradually, everybody began to recognize the young man as a great artist. One day, he made an exceptionally beautiful statue. The king, himself, came to know of it and praised him greatly. But the young artist was not quite happy, for he wanted his father to praise him, too. So he brought the statue to his father, but the father simply said, "Not bad."

"Is that all you can say?"

"It could be much better, son."

The son smashed the statue on the ground, declaring, "Okay, I'm going to do another one!" And with even greater effort, he made another, even more spectacular sculpture. You could almost see the lips move and hear it talk. There was life in it. The whole township came to see it. Everybody was praising it and exclaiming, "Nobody in the world could ever make a statue more beautiful than this." It was really a fantastic work of art.

At this point, the sculptor's son thought: "This time my father won't be able to find anything wrong with my work. I've done a perfect job. There isn't a flaw anywhere." So with all pride and joy, he invited his father to see the statue.

"It's all right, son, but it could still be better."

Then the son went wild. He became furious and shouted at his father, "I worked so hard and did all this, and that is all you can say? You can't even say one word of appreciation? You can't admit it's beautiful? You always say the same thing: 'It could be better! It could be better! It could be better!' I'm tired of it!"

Having said that, the sculptor's son ran away from home and traveled to another country. There he stayed more or less in seclusion. He paid no attention to his physical appearance and even began to look like a crazy man. But he continued to work, wanting to prove that he could create unquestionably beautiful sculptures. During that period, he did a most marvelous work and sent a message to the royal palace inviting the king to come to see it.

The king was curious and sent his minister who was an art lover. The minister saw the statue and exclaimed, "Oh, I have never seen anything like this! The king must see it. Let us bring it to him at once."

The king fell in love with it, too. He told his minister, "Nobody has ever done a piece of work like this. Put it outside in the main square. Let the whole country come and see it."

A large platform was built for the statue, and a festival was held. The king informed everybody, "There's a masterpiece here. Everyone should come and see it." He sent notices all over his country and to the neighboring countries, too.

People came from far and wide and admired the sculpture. Of course, the artist's father, being a sculptor himself, also wanted to see it. So he went, and when he saw the sculpture, he was awestruck. "Ah, even I could not have done this! It's fantastic. Who did this? I would certainly like to meet the artist and offer my congratulations. This sculpture is unequaled."

He just stood in front of the statue, shedding tears of joy. All of a sudden, a madman came running up to him, fell at his feet, and then got up and hugged him. It was his son, who had been hiding in the crowd. When he saw his father's reaction, he was overjoyed and wanted to disclose himself. "Dad, Dad, I am that sculptor. It's me—your son! You've made me *so* happy!"

"My dear son, how are you? What are you doing here? I thought I had lost you."

"Dad, I am the person who made this statue."

There was a long silence. "Well, son, it could have been a little better."

"But I saw you admiring it and saying it's fantastic. Why are you still repeating the same old thing?"

Then the father explained: "Son, if I had admired and appreciated the masterpieces you created years before, you would have stopped there. I wanted you to grow more and more. That's why I kept saying, 'It could be better.' If I'd said it was beautiful then, that would have been the end of your growth."

"Dad, I'm so sorry. Now I understand. Thank you for helping me all these years to become the best that I could be."

If you always hear praise, you become self-satisfied and stop striving. Then your learning ends. We should never be satisfied with our growth. As the proverb says, "What we have learned is just a lump of clay; what we have still to learn is the whole earth itself."

A Drop of Honey

man was walking through the jungle when, all of a sudden, he encountered a large tiger. He was almost exhausted when he saw the tiger, but he was so frightened that he got a burst of adrenaline and started running. The tiger chased after him. The man ran as fast as he could, but all of a sudden, "Whoops!"—he stumbled into a deep, dry well. The well was very old and had been covered over with creepers and vines. Luckily, he didn't fall all the way to the bottom but caught hold of one of the vines.

So there he was hanging midway down the well. He started to climb up, but when he looked up, he saw the tiger standing there. "My gosh," he said, "what should I do now? I can't hold on like this much longer! I'll just have to let go and jump."

As the man was about to jump, he looked down below and saw a big cobra. So there was a cobra below and a tiger above. Just at that moment, the fellow heard a faint scratching noise and felt a vibration along the vine he was holding. He looked up and saw a small rat nibbling on the creeper. At any moment, the creeper would be cut, and he would fall below. What a predicament! He wondered, "What am I to do?"

All of a sudden, something fell onto his lip, a kind of heavy drop. He licked his lip and wondered, "What is that?" Soon he realized that when he fell down, he had disturbed a honeycomb, and a drop of honey now fell onto his lip. "Ah," he thought, "this is just like the honey I had when I went to my mother-in-law's place for the first time and met my wife-to-be. Oh, she was such a beautiful girl." Then he started thinking about his wedding day, the beautiful feast, and how happy the honeymoon had been.

He continued to daydream: "Ah, but unfortunately, she divorced me. Still, she has a sister somewhere. Maybe when I go back, I should ask the sister to marry me." And he started planning for another marriage. Thus, a little, tiny drop of honey made him forget all about the danger of his present situation, as well as his past suffering, and there he was looking to make the same mistakes again in the future.

People constantly think of trifling, temporary, fleeting happiness. They forget all about the knocks and bumps they received in life and make the same mistakes again and again, falling deeper and deeper into the pit. If you want to speed up your growth, learn from your past experiences and stay away from anything that would disturb your peace.

Two Stones

here once was a fellow who went to a mountainside looking for a big rock out of which he could make a sculpture. At last, he found a nice one and brought it home. But after returning home, he realized that the rock was a little too big, so he decided to use only half of it. He split the rock in two and began working on one of the pieces. As soon as he started chiseling, the rock started grumbling, "Hey, stop that! Don't you know that you are hurting me? I was all comfortable before, and now you are chiseling me. Don't touch me anymore!"

The fellow thought, "Maybe this rock has some problem. I'd better leave it alone and try the other half." So he began working on the other half. This one didn't complain at all. In fact, whenever he stopped working, the rock would say, "Why are you stopping? Come on, keep going. I know that you are doing it for my benefit. Please, chip away all the undesirable parts."

Because after all, that is how you make a sculpture from a rock. You don't put a nose here or an eye there; you just chip away all the unnecessary material covering the nose and eye. When all the unnecessary material is removed, you see a beautiful image there. That is why the rock said, "Come on, do it quickly—the sooner the better." And of course, the sculptor was very happy to work with such a rock, one that really appreciated what he was doing.

So the sculptor worked day and night. Soon the sculpture was complete. It was a beautiful image of God, and a temple was built for it. The image was installed, and the priest was about to perform a *puja* and pour milk and honey over it. But he couldn't reach the top of the image, so he looked for something to stand on. He noticed the other rock in the corner and brought it in front of the altar. He stood on the rock and performed the worship.

When the service was over, the priest went home. Then the stone that was lying on the ground looked up and asked the stone that was on the altar, "Hey, brother, what's happening here? The whole day, that fellow was standing on me, trampling me under his feet, while he was pouring milk and honey over you and decorating you with all sorts of beautiful things. How come you are being adored, while I am being trampled on?"

The other stone laughed and said, "Hmm, you still don't seem to realize what has happened. My brother, you could have been here, and I would have been in your place. The sculptor picked you first for the image; but, unfortunately, you didn't want him to touch you. You grumbled. So he left you alone and started working on me. I thought maybe there is something behind all these blows, all this rubbing and scrubbing. I didn't know what he was doing, but somehow I trusted him. And I waited and waited and waited. Slowly, I saw that I was becoming a beautiful image. Happily, I realized that if he hadn't done all that, then I wouldn't be like this today. So you see, I allowed myself to be chiseled and chipped and filed and polished. You didn't like it; you made him stop. Therefore, today you are a steppingstone, and I am here as a deity."

God is like a sculptor; He is trying to bring out the beautiful part in you. Even if the process hurts sometimes, be patient and persevere. In the end, you will come out shining.

The Swami and the Cow

here once was a swami who had a wonderful garden with lots of fruits and vegetables and beautiful flowers all around. One day, a neighbor's cow broke through the fence and ate all the flowers and vegetables that the swami loved so much. The swami really went wild, ran after the cow with a club, and beat the cow until he broke its leg.

When the cow came home, its owner immediately went to the swami and asked, "How could you hit a cow like that and even break its leg? It's an innocent, ignorant animal. It didn't know the garden belonged to you. It simply came and ate. You shouldn't have done that. And I thought you were a spiritual man."

The swami had studied a lot of Vedanta, so immediately he responded, "My son, to whom are you addressing this complaint? *I* didn't do anything. *I* didn't break the cow's leg. I am That I am!"

"Then who broke the leg?"

"This hand broke the leg. *I* am not this hand."

"Then who is responsible for that hand?"

"Don't you know what the scriptures say? There are many deities presiding over the different parts of the body; this hand is presided over by Lord Indra. So Indra functions through this hand, and when this hand hit the cow, Indra was responsible for it."

"Okay, swami," said the neighbor, "I can't argue with you; it's true. I'm sorry. I'll just accept it as the fate of the cow." And he returned home.

Now Indra was watching all of this from his heavenly abode and decided to test the swami. So, the next day, he assumed a disguise and went to visit the garden. "What a lovely garden God has created here," he said.

"What?!" said the swami. "You must be a stranger here. I'm the one who made this garden. Look at my hands! They're covered with calluses. First, I had to dig hundreds of feet to get water. Then, I had to draw all the water myself. For each tree I had to dig a deep hole, and I worked so hard to plant them. It's the hard work that I've done with this very hand that has made this garden grow."

"That's very good," said the visitor, "but I just heard a little while ago that when the hand struck the cow, you blamed Indra. Don't you think that when the hand planted the flower, the credit should also go to Indra?"

"Who are you?" asked the swami.

The stranger immediately assumed his real form and replied, "I am the poor Indra whom you have been blaming for your wrong actions."

The swami immediately got the lesson. "I'm so sorry; please forgive me!" he pleaded. "I will never make this mistake again."

Normally, when anything good happens, we take the credit. But when something bad happens, we try to look for somebody to blame. That kind of "two-way traffic" is not right. You should either take total responsibility for your actions, or else feel that everything is happening according to the will of God.

A Perfect Lie

nce upon a time, there was a hermit who lived in a remote, rural area. He led a very quiet life spent in prayer and meditation. One evening, he was sitting outside his hut when, all of a sudden, he saw a beautiful young girl wearing costly jewels come running toward him crying, "Please, save me! There's somebody chasing me who wants to kill me and steal my jewels! Please let me hide somewhere. . ."

Then, without even waiting for permission, the girl dashed inside his hut. Within a few minutes, a wild-looking man with a dagger in his hand ran up shouting, "Hey! Did you see a girl come this way?" What should the hermit have done? Should he have been honest and said: "I always tell the truth. The girl is hiding inside."

No. Instead, he said, "What girl? My son, can't you see that I'm a hermit? This is no place for young girls."

"Okay," said the man with the dagger, "I'm going that way to look for her." And he ran off in the other direction.

So by the hermit's telling a lie, three lives were saved. The man would have killed the girl and, not wanting to leave the hermit as a witness, would have killed him as well. Moreover, when he went to pawn the jewels, the police would have caught him, and he would have been hanged. Thus, three lives would have been lost had the hermit spoken the truth.

Sometimes even telling a lie can be a selfless and perfect act. If it is going to produce no harm to anybody and at least some benefit to somebody, then even telling a lie is counted as truthfulness. It is the motive and outcome that should be thought of in every action, not just the action itself.

How to Build a Temple

nce there was a powerful and pious king who was proud of both his achievements and his piety. He decided to build the most magnificent temple the country had ever known. So he called on all the best architects and workers, and construction was begun.

As the temple neared completion, the king set a date for its consecration. He prayed earnestly to God to please come and be present at the consecration of this marvelous temple. He was pretty sure that God would come, since there had never been another temple like it in all the land, or even in all the surrounding area. But one night, the Lord appeared to him in a dream and said, "Probably you should pick another day for the ceremony, because I'll be very busy on that one."

"Doing what?" asked the king incredulously.

"I'll be at the consecration of another temple," replied the Lord.

The king was stunned to learn that there was a greater temple than his to be consecrated on the very same day. "Where is this temple?" he asked. And the Lord named the small village in which the temple could be found.

So the king disguised himself and traveled to the village to see this great temple. As he approached, he looked about expecting a high edifice towering above the trees; but he couldn't see anything. He asked a villager, "Is there a great temple here?" The man looked at him as if he were either blind or crazy.

"No, sir, there is nothing here."

"Are you sure? I've been told that there is a great temple in this village."

"You can see there's no temple here. But why don't you ask the swami who lives in a small thatched hut on the edge of town. He's a holy man and will know about temples and the like."

So the king went to the little hut and called to the swami, a poor *sadhu* (spiritual seeker), whose name was Poosalar. "Is there a great temple in this village?" demanded the king. Poosalar shook his head. The king became impatient. "But God has told me that a great temple is to be consecrated here on a particular day," insisted the king.

Poosalar's eyes filled with tears. For a long time, he wept with joy. Then he explained to the king: "I have wanted to build a temple to God for many years. But I am a poor seeker; I have barely enough to eat. So I began to build a great temple in my mind. Each day, I added a stone, carved a pillar, or inlaid some marble. And I invited God to come to the consecration on the very day you have mentioned. Now I know that He will truly come to my temple!"

The king prostrated on the ground before Poosalar. "I, too, have been building a temple to God. But mine has been built with pride, while yours has been built in the heart with love. So, naturally, God chose to come to your temple and not mine."

And afterwards, the king, himself, became a great devotee.

Our acts are judged not by mere outer appearance. God examines our hearts and our inner motives. A perfect act has a pure motive behind it, free from all selfishness and pride.

The Apple Tree

he entire nature demonstrates the joy of giving. Look at an apple tree. It gives us thousands of fruits. If you were to ask the tree, "Hey, how many fruits do you give in a season?" you might hear the following:

"Oh, several thousand."

"Ah, do people come and beg you for them?"

"No, I don't wait for that. I just give."

"Without their even asking?"

"Yes, that's my nature. I find it a joy to give that way."

"What if people throw stones at you? What do you do then?"

"Well, probably those people get even more fruit."

"Suppose nobody comes to take your fruit?"

"That's their business. I don't want to eat my own fruit, so I just drop them."

"But your apples are so delicious. Don't you even want to try one?"

If you have the ears to hear, you will hear the tree laughing at you. "Oh, I'm not like the human beings who eat their own fruit. Only human beings run after their own fruits, and that is why they are so unhappy."

Every thought, every action, bears a fruit. Do not expect that reward for yourself. Instead, live a dedicated life without any selfishness, and you will always retain your peace.

As You Think, So You Become

here was once a spiritual seeker, a *sadhu*, who wanted to spend more time in seclusion. So, he built a nice hermitage on the bank of the river and started doing all his practices there: *japa*, meditation, *pranayama*, and various austerities. After a few months, however, he started noticing something happening on the other side of the river. Many cars were coming and going; lots of people were gathering. And all night long, there seemed to be a lot of fun going on. The *sadhu* became a little curious as to what was happening.

Soon he found out that it was a courtesan's house. Many rich people came in big cars, and they carried on all night. So the *sadhu* began to think, "Gosh, why is she wasting her life like that? Is that why she got a human birth?" He felt very sad, and he started thinking about her more and more. He said, "She shouldn't be doing that; she *really* shouldn't be doing that."

It happened that the courtesan also looked across the river and saw the hermitage and the hermit. She said to herself, "Oh, I don't know why I am leading a dirty life like this. Look at that *sadhu*. He's such a wonderful person—how happy he is, how meditative he is. Oh, I wish *I* had a life like that!"

This kind of thought transference across the river went on for some time. Then it just so happened that the *sadhu* and the courtesan both died suddenly on the same day. Naturally, when death occurs, some friendly spirits come to welcome and receive the soul—just like "birds of a feather flock together." So, all the good, holy spirits from heaven came to the courtesan's house. And all the ugly-looking, ghostly spirits came to the *sadhu's* side of the river.

When the *sadhu* saw all this he asked, "Hey, what's happening? Why are you here? You seem to have gotten your addresses mixed up. Aren't you the spirits from hell?

"Yes, we are from hell," they replied, "and we have come to the right place. That is where you are going."

The *sadhu* was shocked: "Don't you see my hermitage? Don't you know that I'm a hermit? Look at me: I'm just an ordinary, simple fellow with a loincloth. I don't have any luxuries. Look at my *sadhana* chart. I did all my practices regularly—not even one day missed!"

The spirit replied, "Sir, it's true: you did do everything *physically*. And if you look at your body there, it's being treated beautifully with all sorts of rituals. The lady's body, on the other hand, has been left for the vultures. But your mind, unfortunately, was constantly dwelling on the unhappy, ugly life of the lady. You were thinking of her constantly; whereas she was thinking of you all the time, wishing she were like you. So, where you lived and what you did outwardly don't matter so much, because your thoughts were constantly somewhere else. You see, we *have* come to the right place." And with that, the spirits grabbed him and took him to hell, while the lady went to heaven.

As you think, so you become. Your thoughts shape your character and ultimately determine your destiny. That is why it is so important to have pure thoughts.

The Beggar King

ne day, a great king went into the forest to hunt. After some time, he noticed a *sadhu* (spiritual seeker) jumping and dancing and singing. The *sadhu* was wearing only a loincloth. Nearby was the simple thatched hut where he lived. The *sadhu* looked very happy.

The king approached him and asked, "Sir, what makes you so happy?"

"Well, I have God. I am contented. I don't want anything, and so I'm happy."

"Oh," sighed the king. "I would love to see more of your happy face. Would you come with me to the palace? I want to make you an offering."

The *sadhu* said, "What do you want to offer me? I don't need anything."

"You may not need anything, but I would like to offer you something. Will you please come and accept it for my sake?"

"All right. If that's going to make you happy, I'll come with you. Do *you* have everything *you* need?"

"Oh, yes. I am a wealthy king; I have everything."

"Is that so? Okay, let us go then." And he followed the king to the palace.

When they entered the palace, the king wanted to show the holy man that he was also a great devotee—not just an ordinary king—so he brought the *sadhu* to his beautiful, well-decorated shrine room. After they entered, the king said, "This is the time for my noon worship. Please be seated. I'll just finish my prayers, and then I'll show you the rest of the palace."

"Okay. Fine."

The king made the *sadhu* sit in a place where he could comfortably see the king performing the *puja* at the altar. The king wanted to show what a wonderful *puja* he could do.

48

(Oftentimes that happens: people worship as a show for others, secretly wishing others will say, "Oh, look at that wonderful *puja!*" They take great pains to repeat all the prayers or chants just right. But God isn't concerned with that. God doesn't care what language you pray in or what words you use. He wants to see how pure your heart is, how sincere you are.)

The king's *puja* took almost three hours—with a lot of flowers, fruit, incense, and waving of lights. After the *puja,* it's customary to appeal to God for anything that you need in life. So when the king finished the worship, he prayed, "Lord, You have given me everything. By Your Grace, I have plenty. There is only one thing that is bothering me. That king in the little country next door—I feel threatened by his presence. If only I could take over that country and absorb it into my territory, everything would be fine. Please, Lord, grant me that boon." He finished his plea and prostrated on the floor before the altar.

When the king got up, he saw the *sadhu* walking out. The king ran after him. "Swami, swami! You are going away. I haven't even offered you anything. I'm sorry. I probably made you wait too long while I did the *puja,* but that's the way I do it every day."

"No, no, no. There is nothing wrong with your *puja*. The problem is, I don't like to receive anything from beggars."

"What do you mean? Are you saying that I am a beggar?"

"Yes. What else were you doing there in the shrine room? You told me that you had everything, yet there you were, begging for another country to be added to yours. How can you give anything to me? I already have everything, while you are still living in want."

The king immediately realized his mistake and fell at the feet of the *sadhu.*

"Swamiji, I understand now," said the king. "This is the end of my wants. I renounce everything. Please let me follow you."

The ministers came to try to stop the king, but he calmly told them, "Somebody else can take care of the kingdom; I am finished with all that." And he followed the *sadhu* out of the palace.

Contentment is golden. If the mind is distracted by desires, it's impossible to know God. It's only when the mind is calm, clear, and unruffled by desires that you can experience that Supreme Peace.

The Butcher and the Yogi

 spiritual seeker named Kausika was meditating under a tree when he felt something fall onto his shoulder. He wanted to know the source of the disturbance and looked up to see a bird sitting on the branch above him. It was the bird's excrement that had fallen on him. Immediately, he became angry. "How dare you do this to me!" he exclaimed as he glared at the bird. And as he stared, flames leapt from his eyes and burned the poor little bird to ash. "Aha," he thought, "I have really attained some special powers. My meditation has been fruitful."

At noon, as was his habit, he walked to a nearby village to beg for some food. He stood before the house where he often got alms, but that day his tone was a little different. He called out, "Give me some food!"

Immediately, the woman inside noticed the change. "Excuse me, sir; I'm busy right now, but I'll come as soon as I can."

"Doesn't this woman know who I am?" thought Kausika. "How dare she make me wait!"

After a short while, the woman came to the door with the food. "You know, sir," she said, "I'm not a bird for you to burn."

He almost fainted. "What did you say? How do you know what happened in the forest? I haven't told anybody."

"You don't need to; you are reflected clearly in my mind."

"You can't be an ordinary housewife. What kind of *sadhana* (spiritual practice) do you do? Do you have a special mantra? You seem to have much greater powers than I."

"I don't know any mantras. I'm just a housewife, and I take care of my sick husband who is bedridden. When you came, I was attending him. That's why I asked you to wait. I'm doing my duty in taking care of my husband. God placed me in this position, and I'm fulfilling my responsibilities as best I can. That's all there is to tell."

"That's *all* you do? I want to know more."

"Please, I'm not a scholar. I can't say anything more. If you want, go to the next town and seek out a butcher there by the name of Vyadhan. He will tell you more."

"A butcher? You really want me to go to a *butcher*?"

"He's the one to answer your questions."

Kausika was really curious now, so he journeyed to the next town. As he approached the butcher shop, he saw a big fellow with a huge knife, chopping and bargaining, haggling with customers over every penny. "He looks and sounds like a demon," thought Kausika. "How is he going to teach me anything?"

He was considering leaving when Vyadhan looked up and called to him, "Ah, so you have come. The lady in the next village sent you. Please have a seat. I'll finish my job soon, and then we can talk."

Kausika was stunned. The butcher seemed to know everything. So Kausika sat quietly waiting. He saw that Vyadhan was not an easy businessman to deal with. He was strict about his prices; he never gave in to anybody.

When everything was finished, Vyadhan closed the shop and called to Kausika, "Come on, let's go home." On the way, Vyadhan purchased some vegetables. "Please sit," he said. "I'll just cook these vegetables and feed my parents. They're old and blind, too. I need to take care of them. But as soon as I'm finished, we can talk."

A little while later, Vyadhan returned and said, "Now, let me make something for you to eat, and then we'll talk."

"No, I'm not interested in eating. My hunger is different. Please feed me with your wisdom instead. I don't understand anything. I used to think that by sitting under a tree and repeating a mantra I was doing *sadhana*. And I did get something from my practice. But you people are doing all kinds of things. You are a butcher, and she is a housewife. Yet you seem to have achieved much more than I. You seem to know everything that I have in mind—and probably much more, too. How is that possible?"

Then Vyadhan explained: "I believe in God. God created everything and everybody. He is the very life force functioning through you and me and everything. We are all His gadgets; He is the main current. He gave me two elderly parents to care for. He made me a butcher and gave me this duty to do. So I do my duty, knowing all the while that it is really Him doing it through me. That's all I know. I'm not doing anything for my sake; I'm doing everything for the sake of others. I do it all as Karma Yoga, as service, so my mind is always calm and clean. There are no disturbances in my mind. You scholarly people might say I'm a yogi. All I know is that the Truth is always clearly reflected in my peaceful mind."

If you always do your duty as selfless service to God and the creation, your mind will retain its peace, and you will realize the Truth.

The Saint and the Scorpion

ne day, a holy woman went to a river to bathe and found that the river was in flood. As she approached the rushing water, she saw a scorpion being carried away by the current. She took pity on it and thought, "Oh, it is going to die." So she reached forward and took the scorpion out of the water. While she was taking it out, the scorpion stung her hand. As she got stung, she jumped, and the scorpion fell back into the water. Again she felt pity: "Oh, I'm so sorry. No, I will not let you die." She lifted the scorpion again, got another sting, and again dropped it.

A friend was standing behind her watching the whole scene. As the woman reached in to take the scorpion out of the water one more time, the friend said, "Every time you pick up the scorpion, it stings you. Why do you continue to pick it up? Have you no common sense?"

"Well," said the woman, "I don't know about common sense. All I know is that my nature is to feel pity for something, to be compassionate, and if possible, to save it. That is just the way I am."

The friend replied, "But don't you see that the scorpion is stinging you and will continue to sting you?"

The saintly woman explained, "What can I do? That is its nature. I cannot change its nature. And in the same way, you cannot change my nature."

We should accept things as they are, people as they are, without demanding anything. Our love should be unconditional.

The Man Who Overcame Anger

nce a spiritual seeker went into seclusion in a cave and stayed there for almost ten years. He didn't see anyone in all that time. People used to come and leave food for him, and when they left, he would eat it. After ten years, one day he decided to come out and see everyone. Everybody came running to his cave. "Sir," they eagerly asked, "by sitting in the cave these ten years, what did you gain?"

He replied, "Years ago, I used to be very angry. Every little thing would disturb me. But for the past ten years, I've had no anger at all. I have overcome anger. That is a big achievement."

Someone got up and said, "Sir, how can you remember all that happened for the past ten years? Maybe one day you might have become a little angry."

"No, not at all. Not even once did I get angry."

Another fellow stood up. "Sir, it is really hard to believe. Are you sure that there wasn't *one* time when you were angry?"

Impatiently, the man replied, "Absolutely not!"

Still another person asked, "Really? Didn't you even feel *slightly* angry?"

Now he roared: "Never! Never! Never! You fool, didn't you hear me? I said I have totally conquered anger!"

When there is nobody to irritate you, it's easy to be peaceful. You should have ample opportunities to get disturbed, and if you still remain peaceful, only then will you have proved that you have achieved something.

The Wedding Guest

nce a fellow received an invitation to a wedding party. He went to the party very simply dressed. But the host happened to be a rich man, so all the other guests were very elegantly dressed. When the fellow arrived, the gatekeeper stopped him and demanded, "Hey, who are you? Where do you think you're going?" Everyone just stared at the fellow. In fact, even the owner of the house pretended not to recognize him.

So, the fellow went back home, borrowed an expensive suit, and returned to the party. Immediately, the same gatekeeper said, "Please, please come in. Our master has been looking for you. Where did you go? What happened to you? Please come this way." And he escorted him to the dinner table.

The man sat down, and when everybody started eating, he picked up his food and began throwing it all over himself. He took a little pudding and rubbed it on his jacket; he took some bread and stuffed it in his pocket; he poured the soup on his pants. "Hey, what are you doing? Are you crazy?" asked the other guests.

"Oh, no; of course not. I'm just eating."

"That's not the way to eat!"

"Yes, but when I came before, dressed in my usual way, nobody would feed me. Now, when I am dressed like this, everybody is ready to host me. So, obviously, the food is being offered to the clothes, not to me."

Often we judge others in a very superficial way. Our sense of beauty is based on their dress, their makeup, and their hairdo. But that is not the real beauty. Real beauty comes from purity of heart, from a well-balanced mind that shows no bias. We should develop that inner cosmic beauty and not depend on the cosmetic beauty.

The Imitation Saint

 there once was a thief who sneaked into the royal palace at night in order to rob the queen's jewels. He was just about to break into her jewel case when he heard footsteps approaching. He quickly hid himself under the bed, and not a moment too soon, for just then the king and queen entered the royal bed chamber.

"I'm very worried about our daughter," the queen said to her husband. "It's high time that she got married, but she refuses to marry anyone except a *sannyasi*. She says that she will only marry a holy man!"

"Don't worry," said the king. "Tomorrow, I will send my minister to the temple to find a holy man for her to wed."

"No swami is interested in householder life," said the queen.

"Well, there must be *one*," said the king, "and we shall find him, and he will become our son-in-law!"

Meanwhile, the thief under the bed got an idea. "All I have to do is go to the temple tomorrow and pretend to be a holy man, and half the kingdom will be mine!"

As soon as he was sure the king and queen were asleep, he fled from the palace. He didn't even bother to take any of the queen's jewels; he had a better plan now.

Early the next morning, the thief wrapped an orange cloth around his waist and went to the temple. He carefully observed how the real swamis sat and behaved so that he could give a convincing imitation.

Soon, the king's minister approached the temple. He went before the *sannyasis*, one by one, and very respectfully bowed down before each of them in turn. The thief was a little worried, because he thought any one of them might accept the king's proposition. He couldn't imagine why a swami would not be willing to give up his poor, solitary life for such a reward. What was so wonderful in a renunciate's life that he would prefer that over family, wealth, and power?

Some of the swamis flatly refused and went back to their meditation. The rest didn't even bother to open their eyes. The minister was getting discouraged, but he had to fulfill his duty, so he kept on going. Finally, he approached the thief. The thief straightened up, shut his eyes, and tried as best he could to look like all of the other swamis he had seen meditating. After about five minutes, he began to wonder what had happened to the minister. Slowly, he opened his eyes and saw the minister patiently waiting a few feet in front of him. The minister bowed down, touching his very head to the ground before the thief, just as he had with the real swamis.

"Forgive me, Swamiji," he said. "I hope I did not disturb your meditation."

"No, you did not disturb me," answered the thief. "What is it you would like me to do for you?"

The minister asked the thief to take the princess in marriage, thereby receiving half the kingdom and one day being crowned king himself. The thief did not want to appear too anxious for fear that the minister might suspect him. So he looked thoughtful for a minute and then said: "I don't know. I'm very happy like this, but I would like to oblige the king. Why don't you come back tomorrow, and I will give you my answer then."

The minister was overjoyed and, as a token of encouragement, left a bag full of gold coins for the pseudo-swami.

That night, the minister reported to the king. He told the king about what a hard time he had had at the temple, but that there was one swami who might be persuaded.

"Can you think of any way we might be able to influence his decision?" asked the king.

"Well, perhaps if you were to come with me and speak to him yourself."

"Very well. I shall do it!"

The next day, the thief again sat by the temple. Soon the minister came by, but this time the king, the queen, and the beautiful princess were all with him. All four bowed down before the thief. The king, himself, extended the invitation to the swami, offering him his daughter, half his kingdom, and the promise to be heir to the throne.

The thief had intended to accept the minister's offer, but here was the king, himself, speaking to him. Now he thought: "My goodness! Just for *acting* like a *sannyasi*, the princess, the royal minister, the king, and the queen all are at my feet. Even for imitating—imagine if I were to become a real *sannyasi* . . ."

So he said, "I'm sorry, Your Majesty. I would like to serve you, but I must refuse your offer. I do not wish to give up this simple life. Don't even bother to come this way anymore. Nobody here is going to be tempted by your offer!"

The thief started out by just imitating the real spiritual seekers, but in the end, he became one himself. Good company, or satsanga, *is that powerful. Just by keeping the right company, one can obtain spiritual liberation.*

The Golden Mongoose

here's a beautiful story in the *Mahabharata*, a great religious epic from India, that tells of the noble Pandava family. At one time, the Pandavas were conducting a great *yagna,* or ritual sacrifice. The *yagna* was done with all pomp and show, and at great expense. Many people came and were enjoying it very much. As they were sitting and appreciating it, they saw a strange-looking mongoose suddenly come running toward them. It immediately started rolling in the remnants of the food and other offerings. Then it stood up and said, "Humph!" while shaking itself off, looking completely disappointed.

The guests rose and asked, "What is this? You don't look like an ordinary mongoose. You seem to be a little peculiar: one half of your body is a golden color, while the other half is ordinary mongoose color. Will you tell us why this is so?"

"Oh, that's a long story," the mongoose said. "I don't know if it's worth telling."

"Please tell us. We want to know."

"Okay, because you are asking, I'll tell you. I was just an ordinary mongoose before, without this golden color. One day, as I was roaming around, I came across a small hut. I sat outside for a while and watched what was happening within.

"A poor teacher and his wife were living there with their son and daughter-in-law. At that time, there was a terrible famine in the land. Food was very scarce, and they didn't have anything to eat. Fortunately, one of the teacher's former students had brought a little flour to be cooked into *rotis,* a kind of flat bread. So the wife started preparing it.

"When everything was ready, the teacher came out of the house and looked this way and that to see if anybody was coming. This was his custom, because the scriptures say: *'Atithi devo bhava,'* which means 'treat the guest as God.' God comes in the form of the guest. And that day, the teacher did see somebody coming. So he said, 'Sir, would you like to have some food?'

"'Oh, sure. I'm really hungry.'

"So they went inside. From the flour, the wife had made four *rotis*, one for each person. The teacher gave his share to the guest, who finished it.

"Then the wife came and said, 'Sir, may I offer you another?'

"'Oh, sure, sure. I don't know why, but I'm terribly hungry today.' So he ate that one also.

"Then the son and daughter-in-law, who had been watching, came with their shares. 'Sir, we would like to offer these also, if you can eat them.'

"'I think I can.' He ate their bread also and said, 'Thank you so much. God bless you all.' Then he just walked out. Within half an hour, all four of them collapsed and died because they were in such terrible hunger—but they died in joy.

"I was watching all this. I was also a little hungry, so I went in to see if any crumbs had fallen while the woman was making the bread. I saw a little flour on the floor. It was not even fit for eating, so I just rolled in it. When I got up, I saw half of my body had become golden, and I thought: 'Oh, there's something mysterious and miraculous here, something divine in their actions. Yes, certainly, they have sacrificed their lives for the sake of another. They have done a beautiful *yagna*.'

"Then, somehow, I got this kind of crazy idea: 'How am I going to make the other half of my body also golden?' So ever since that day, I've been rolling around everywhere. Then, I heard that Yudhishthira, the great Pandava, was doing a big *yagna*, and I thought, 'Certainly, this will be much greater than the offering of those four poor people.' So, I came running all the way here. But, unfortunately, it didn't work."

You should have seen Yudhishthira's face! In the Pandava *yagna*, there was sacrifice, but it was probably mingled with a little pride. But those four simple people had true humility.

What is really important is the quality of heartfulness in our actions—not the outer pomp and show. If our actions have that spirit of dedication, they are truly divine.

The Demon Who Was Turned to Ash

fellow, who later came to be known as Basmasura, or the Ash Demon, went to Mt. Kailash and started meditating on Lord Siva. He practiced there for several years, and his mind became very one-pointed. Because of his power of concentration, Lord Siva appeared to him and said, "I am satisfied with your concentration. Ask for whatever boon you want, and I will grant it."

Basmasura replied, "If ever I put my hand on somebody's head, immediately that person will be turned into a pile of ash. That is the boon I want."

Lord Siva asked, "Are you sure that's what you want?"

And Basmasura replied, "Absolutely!"

"Okay, you want it, you got it." As Lord Siva turned to go, Basmasura called him back. "What do you want now?" asked Lord Siva. "You got what you asked for."

"I just want to test the power to make sure that I really have it. Since there's nobody else around, I would like to test it on you."

Having given the power to Basmasura, Lord Siva had no authority to take it back. So He had to run for His life, with Basmasura close behind. Lord Siva wanted someone to rescue Him, so He thought of His counterpart, Lord Vishnu, who is the protector, and called to Him for help.

Immediately, Lord Vishnu appeared and transformed himself into a very beautiful girl. Basmasura was running as fast as he could to catch Lord Siva, but as soon as he saw the girl, he stopped in his tracks. "Hey, who are you? Where are you going? Are you single?" he asked with all eagerness.

"Certainly," she replied, "why else would I be here all alone?"

"Can I accompany you then? Can I be your friend? Can I give you a little hug?"

"Well, I do like you," she said, "and you seem quite nice, but your hair is a little wild and it's scaring me away."

"Oh! What is wrong with my hair? It should be all right." And with that, Basmasura placed his hands on his head and was immediately turned to ash. He had forgotten to exclude himself when he requested his boon. Such a terrible heat was produced when he burned that the earth started boiling. Even today, there is a great hot water stream running at the spot where Basmasura was turned to ash.

Purity of heart is not the same as one-pointedness of mind. Even evil-minded people can concentrate and attain great powers, but such powers won't be helpful if your mind is not clean. So, refine your body and mind, and let the power awaken naturally at the proper time. Then you will be a beautiful instrument in the hands of the Divine.

The Milkmaid

here was once a milkmaid who supplied milk to an ashram. She came from a neighboring village and had to cross a big river to get there, so she used to deliver the milk by boat. One rainy day she was very late. The swami in charge was looking for some milk, and when he didn't find any, he asked his assistant what had happened. "The milkmaid hasn't come today," the assistant replied.

"Why not?" asked the swami.

"I don't know; we're still waiting for her," said the assistant.

Two hours later the milkmaid arrived, and the swami casually asked her, "Why are you late today? You usually come so punctually."

"Oh, the river was flooded. So I had to wait until the water subsided a little, and the boatman felt it safe enough to bring us across."

Then the swami jokingly said, "Aha, what is this? You come here, bring me milk, and sometimes even sit and listen to my talk. By that alone, people cross the big ocean of life. Can't you cross this little river?"

"Oh, I'm so sorry! I never thought of that. I will remember it from now on." And with those words, the milkmaid returned to her village.

The rain continued to pour. So the next day, they expected her to be late again, but she arrived at the usual time. And every day thereafter, she was equally punctual. The swami wondered how she could continue to be so punctual when the river was still in flood. So he questioned her, and she replied: "Swami, you taught me the trick. Now I know how to cross. I don't need to wait for the boat."

"What?!"

"Yes, Swami, I don't need to wait for the boat."

"Then how do you come?"

"I just think of you, the guru, and walk across."

"You really walk on the water?"

"Yes."

"*On* the water?"

"Not exactly. The water actually comes up to my ankles, but it does not go any farther. See? The hem of my dress didn't even get wet."

The swami became very suspicious. "I'd like to see that for myself."

"Sure. Why not? Come on; I have to go back now anyway."

So they went down to the riverbank. The milkmaid started walking across the river and called to the swami, "Come on, come on." The swami was a little hesitant, but he thought that maybe somehow it would work if he tried it, so he stepped into the water. As he began to walk, the water started rising up around him. "Swami," the milkmaid said, "just by thinking of your name, I am walking over the water, and you can't walk on it yourself?"

"Child," he said, "I am only a ladder. I can help others go up, but I can't go up myself. You have faith, and so you are able to walk across. But I don't have such pure, childlike faith." He turned and went back, feeling so ashamed that he was just a scholar and that even though he had learned much philosophy, he still had not realized the Truth.

God can't be experienced just by talking philosophy. God is the simplest thing in life and should be approached in a simple way. The simplest way is to just have faith.

The Boy Who Made God Eat His Pudding

any years ago in South India, there lived a very orthodox *Brahmin*. Every day he spent several hours in his morning worship. He had a beautiful altar, and he used to perform a big *puja* (worship service) there. At the same time, there was a little weakness in his mind. He was very fond of a certain kind of pudding. Unfortunately, his financial situation was such that he couldn't afford to have the pudding all the time. But he was so keen on having it, that he thought of a little trick to get some every day.

Normally during a *puja*, when the food is offered to God, a curtain is drawn in front of the altar to allow God to enjoy the food by Himself. Then, after a little while, the *pujari* will go in and bring out the blessed food to share with everyone. So the man used to ask his wife to make a little pudding to offer to God at the morning *puja*. But when he went behind the curtain, he would eat the food himself, and then come out and tell the family that God had accepted his worship and had eaten the pudding. Everybody in the family was so happy because they thought that every day God came and ate their offering.

Thus it continued for many months. Then one day, it so happened that the man had to go to a distant village for an important occasion. Because he was an orthodox *Brahmin*, he still wanted the daily worship at his home to take place. So he called his little boy, who used to help him with the *puja*, and said, "Son, you have seen how I have been doing the *puja*. I won't be able to do it today, so I would like you to do it."

The son replied, "Okay, Dad. I'll be happy to do it."

So the father left, and the son began the *puja*. As usual, the mother brought a little pudding and gave it to the son to offer to God. At the appropriate time during the *puja*, the son placed the pudding on the altar, closed the curtain, and went out to wait while God ate the pudding. After a little while, the boy went to remove the bowl and, to his horror, he saw that the pudding was still there. He thought, "I must have done something terribly wrong. God is not happy with my *puja*; that is why He refused to eat the pudding today. I thought I was doing the *puja* exactly like my dad." Then he cried out to God, "Please, God, if my father finds out that I made You starve, he will be so angry with me. Please eat the pudding!"

Then the boy placed the bowl down again, closed the curtain, and went out to wait. When he returned, the bowl was still full. He fell in front of the altar and started crying, "God, if You don't eat the pudding today, and if my dad comes and finds out, he's going to kill me! *Please*, eat it!"

He checked again, and the pudding was still there. This time, he started crying so hard that he fainted. After half an hour, when he came to, he saw that the bowl was empty. He started jumping with joy. "Oh, God, I'm so happy. You heard my prayer. Now I can tell my dad that You accepted my worship, too!"

The son eagerly awaited his father's return. His father finally came back very late that evening. As soon as the boy saw him walking up to the house, he ran to meet him, saying, "Dad, Dad, God accepted my worship, too! He ate the pudding just as He does for you every day. At first He refused, but then I cried and cried and cried and *made* Him eat it!"

Of course, the father thought that, somehow, the boy had known all along what he was doing and had simply been waiting for an opportunity to do the same thing himself. So he questioned him, "Are you *sure* that God ate the pudding?"

"Yes, Dad, there's no doubt about it!"

"All right. In that case, you can do the *puja* tomorrow, also. I'd like to see it."

"Okay, Dad. If God ate the pudding today, why shouldn't He eat it tomorrow, too?"

The next day the boy did the *puja*, but God didn't eat the pudding. So the boy started crying again. He was almost ready to dash his head on the floor, but at that point, a voice came: "Son, don't cry. I would like to accept your offering, but I can't do so in front of your father. He doesn't deserve to see me eat it. That's why I didn't eat it right away."

The father also heard the voice. Then he fell at the feet of his child and said, "You are my guru; you've opened my eyes. I wish I had the faith and devotion that you have. I'm just a scholar. I did the *puja* correctly according to the scriptures, but I didn't have the kind of innocent faith that you have. That is why God never really ate the pudding that I offered Him, but He accepted yours."

Even knowing all the scriptures by heart will not bring God's grace. God doesn't care how much you know; He wants your pure heart. A sincere prayer from a pure, faithful heart will never go unanswered.

You Are What You Eat

ne day in India, a swami was invited to a rich man's house for lunch. Normally, when a swami goes out, a few disciples go with him. So they all went there and had a sumptuous lunch. It was served on beautiful silver plates with silver cutlery, because the host was a very rich man. At the end of the meal, the swami blessed the man and his family, said good-bye, and left the house with his disciples.

They had been walking for about half a mile when one disciple, the youngest one, came running up to the swami.

"Swamiji, I've made a terrible mistake!"

The swami asked him, "Why? What did you do?"

"I'm even ashamed to tell you, because I have never done anything like this before!"

"It's all right," the swami answered. "Don't worry; just tell me."

The disciple's hand was shaking as he pulled a silver spoon from his pocket. "I took this from the man's house," he confessed.

The swami smiled at him and said, "All right, you are still young; you are a beginner in spiritual practice. You will become strong as time goes on. Now, take it back and apologize; we will wait for you."

The other disciples questioned the swami: "Why were you so lenient with him? Don't you think you should be more strict?"

The swami said, "Not this time. You see, it is not entirely his mistake."

"He stole the spoon, and you say it's not his mistake! How can that be?" they asked.

Finally, the swami explained: "Do you know the rich man who fed us? He was formerly a banker, and he used to overcharge his customers. So in a way, he is a thief. When he fed us with his food, the vibrations of a thief also came with the food. You are all a little older and stronger, so it did not affect you. But the youngest disciple was affected by that vibration, and so he took the spoon."

You are what you eat! The vibrations with which food comes to you will affect you. See that your food is clean and that it comes to you from a good source.

How To Stop an Elephant

nce upon a time, there lived a king who had a very big elephant. An attendant used to take the elephant to the river every day for a bath. Normally, when an elephant walks, it is restless, and with its trunk, grabs all kinds of things that it sees on the roadside. An elephant can be very difficult to control.

One day, as the attendant was bringing the elephant back to the palace, a little boy came walking up to it. He took its trunk in his hands and said, "Stop! Look at the way you are walking!" The elephant stopped. "Walk gently, carefully," he told the elephant. He let go of the trunk, and the elephant started walking calmly away. The next day, as the elephant passed the same spot, the boy came running and stopped the elephant to reprimand it again. This happened several days in a row.

The attendant couldn't believe what was happening. He told the king, who sent his minister to check on the boy. In a few days, the minister reported back to the king. "Sir, I have observed the boy. He lives with his grandmother. He's just a normal little boy. He seems ordinary, but he has absolutely no fear. That's why he can stop your elephant."

"I can't believe it," said the king. "What do you mean?"

"Sir, a mind without fear and worry can do anything."

The king wanted the minister to prove his point. The only way to do so was to make the boy worry about something. So the minister went to see the boy's grandmother. After learning from her that the boy was allowed to do anything he wanted, the minister asked, "Has he ever asked for anything and been refused?"

"No. I have given him everything he has ever wanted. He is just a happy-go-lucky boy."

"Is he afraid of anything?"

"Nothing at all."

The minister had to prove his theory to the king, so he said, "All right. When your grandson comes home today, give him the usual food but add less than the usual amount of salt. If he asks about it, tell him that you don't have enough money to buy salt, so you had to be sparing with what you have left."

The grandmother said, "If that's what the king wants me to do, I shall do it."

That evening when the boy came home, the grandmother served his supper right away. After a few bites, the boy said, "Grandma, what's wrong? The food's not tasty today." The grandmother repeated what the minister had told her, and the boy said, "Okay, Grandmother, I will get you some salt."

He ran to the shop and asked the shopkeeper to give him a little salt. The shopkeeper explained that he couldn't give him salt without receiving money in exchange.

"Where can I get some money?" asked the boy.

"You have to go to work for it."

"I don't know how to work."

"Then you can't get any salt."

The boy returned home a little depressed. "Grandma, I don't know what to do. The shopkeeper wants me to go to work to get money before he will give me some salt. I don't know how to work."

"All right, sweetheart," said the grandmother; "it doesn't matter. Go to sleep. We'll talk about it tomorrow."

The boy went to bed, but he couldn't sleep at all that night. In the morning, the elephant came as usual; and as usual, the boy went to stop the elephant, but he couldn't do it. The elephant pushed him aside and walked off. All the young fellow had in mind was, "I can't get a little salt for my food." That one small worry was enough to take away all his strength.

Never worry about anything. Worry doesn't bring any benefit to anyone. On the other hand, it saps your energy and takes away whatever capacity you do have. Instead, remain calm and peaceful, and you will always know what to do.

The Greedy Milkman

here was once a milkman who lived in a village where he kept a couple of cows. He used to milk the cows and then take the milk to the next village to sell. But over time, he slowly became greedy and began adding water to the milk. He gradually added more and more water until he had doubled the amount. If he had one gallon of milk, he would add one gallon of water, and then sell it as two gallons of milk.

The milkman did that for a long time, and finally the day came for him to collect all the money. It came to 1000 rupees. As he was returning to his village, it started to rain. The river was flooded, so he tied the money to himself very securely and started slowly wading across. As he reached the middle, he slipped and fell down; but somehow, he managed to swim to the other shore. Immediately, he reached for his money. He opened the bundle and started counting. There were only 500 rupees! He had lost 500 in the river.

The milkman was sitting there very broken-hearted when a wise man approached. "What happened?" asked the wise man. "You look so sad and dejected." So the milkman explained how he had lost his money crossing the river.

"Aha," said the wise man, "I understand now. You are a milkman. Don't worry; you still have your milk money. The water money went to the water; the milk money came with you."

It's not how much you make, but how you make it that is important. If ever you lose money all of a sudden, know that it was ill-earned money. Well-earned money will bring you health and happiness; ill-earned money never can.

You Can Have It All

nce a king decided to test his ministers. He asked them to bring all his possessions to a park and arrange a big exhibition. There were many beautiful and valuable things. They put a throne right in the middle, and once he was seated, the king announced: "Before the sun sets, everyone may come and select whatever they want. But no one may leave the compound until I give permission to do so."

Everybody ran to the park, and each one took something. While they were picking and choosing, a peasant woman walked in. Everyone looked up as they were curious to see what she would take. She walked over to the king and said, "Sir, I heard your offer. Are you sure you are willing to give me *anything* within the compound?"

"Yes, why do you question me?"

"I just wanted to make sure."

"Yes. You may ask for anything in the park that you want."

"Well, sir, I want you."

Everybody was shocked. "How dare she!" they exclaimed.

Then the king explained: "I, too, am inside the compound. All you people chose my things, but she chose me. Whoever takes the king, automatically gets his kingdom. Then he turned to the woman and said, "Yes, I am yours and so, too, is everything that belongs to me."

Don't run after little, trifling things. Find the peace within, which is the image of God in you, and you will have everything. As the Holy Bible says, "Seek ye first the kingdom of God, and all else shall be added unto you."

The Conference on Light

nce upon a time, there was a big meeting in a candle factory. All the candles gathered and were wondering why they were made. One of the candles said, "Why, certainly, our purpose is to give light. We should have a big conference on light to discuss how that can be done."

So, all the candles came and read papers about light and how good it is to get enlightened. But, unfortunately, they were having the conference in total darkness, because not one of the candles was lit. So, after having spent many hours in darkness discussing the light, one little candle got tired. "What kind of conference is this anyway?" it asked. "We are not getting anywhere; we are simply talking on and on. Let me go out for a little fresh air."

So, it left the room. As it was walking down the hall, it noticed some light shining in a corner. "Oh," the little candle cried, "we are just talking about light, but there actually seems to be some light over there. Let me go see."

It slowly walked toward the light and saw another candle sitting there. "Sir," the little candle said, "how did you get light?"

The lit candle smiled and said, "Well, if you really want to know, I will tell you. I was once an unlit candle just like you. But one day, I found a lit candle. I just went and rubbed myself against it. As I rubbed, I caught a spark and got lit."

"Oh," said the little candle, "could I do that with you?"

"Sure, that would be fine."

"But, sir, I don't want to take away any of your light."

"Don't worry about that," said the lit candle. "By your getting light, I will not lose any light. I will still be the same."

The little candle got very excited. "Should I worship you, sir?" he asked. "Should I burn some incense or get a nice garland?"

"You don't need to do all that," said the lit candle. "Just come and rub. You can be grateful to me, but first come and get the light."

So the little candle mustered up all its strength and courage, and slowly approached the lit candle. It caught a spark and cried out in joy, "Now, I have light, too. And you still have the same luminosity. You didn't lose anything!"

"That's what I told you would happen," explained the candle.

"Oh, sir," said the little candle, "there are so many thousands of unlit candles out there. Can I go rub against them?"

"Sure, you can do that now. You are just like me; there is no difference any more. Go ahead."

The little candle slowly returned to the conference room. A heated argument about light was still going on, but the moment the others saw the candle, they all stopped talking.

"Hey," they called out, "where did you get that light? Can we get some, too?"

The candle told them the whole story and finished by saying, "Anyone who wants light, come rub against me."

Immediately, they all came forward and rubbed against the little candle. At last, the conference on light was filled with light!

Simply having conferences about peace when there is no peace in your heart will never bring peace to the world. If you want to share something with others, you must first have it yourself. Find the peace within, and your mere presence will bring peace to others.

Two Boatmen

ave you heard the story of the two boatmen? They knew how to row, but they didn't own a boat. One day, they decided to steal a boat so they could go to the neighboring village. They waited until nightfall and then went down to the river. To celebrate their adventure, they first had a little to drink. In fact, they became quite intoxicated. Then they found a boat, took hold of the oars, and started rowing. They sang and rowed all night long.

Slowly the dawn came, and they could see people approaching the river to bathe. As the people drew nearer, one of the boatmen remarked, "That's strange, these people seem familiar; they look just like the people in our village!"

The other boatman said, "All the buildings look familiar, too! Hey! We seem to be in the same place! What happened?"

The bathers asked, "What do you mean, 'what happened?' What were you two trying to do?"

The boatmen replied, "We wanted to visit the next village and planned to return very soon. So, we just borrowed the boat. We have been rowing the whole night. We can't understand why we are still here."

"You fools!" exclaimed the bathers. "You forgot to untie the knot. All the while you were tied to the shore. You may have rowed all night, but you didn't go anywhere!"

To attain success in Yoga, you need both practice and non-attachment. You may practice a lot, but if you don't renounce selfish attachments, you will never reach the goal.

A Stone for God

here is a story of a devotee of Lord Siva named Sakkiya. He was a complete fool, and yet he came to be revered as a saint. One day Sakkiya said, "Everybody goes and worships God with all sorts of offerings: they pour milk, honey, ghee, and yogurt; they gently place flowers before His image. Why do people use all these items? They say that God is above all these things. All right; I'm going to worship Him with a stone. Every day, I'm going to take a stone and throw it at His image, and let me see whether God is going to bless me and reveal Himself to me or not."

Sakkiya proceeded to do just that. He even vowed, "I will not take food in the morning until I have thrown a stone at Him. That will be my worship!" It was a common practice not to take food before worship, because when the stomach is heavy, you can't worship well. That is one reason why people fast on special occasions. So Sakkiya vowed, "I will throw a stone as worship to God. Only then, will I eat." And he did that every day.

But one day something happened. Sakkiya couldn't find a stone. He looked everywhere—he found only huge rocks that he couldn't lift. He ran everywhere, but failed to find a stone. It was a big test, but still he stuck to his vow. Days passed; his stomach would not keep quiet. It was pinching him. After going without water or food for so many days, he became very weak. "What a fool I am," he said. "I don't know why I made this vow. Still, I should stick to it. But, O God, I am dying. . ." And as he said that, in desperation, he clasped his head between his hands. "What is this?" Every day his hands had picked up stones, so they knew the feeling well—something hard and round.

The minute he felt his head between his hands, he thought, "Ah, here is a stone." He forgot it was his head. He immediately began twisting it. He didn't even care about his own life anymore. His only concern was that he had to have a stone to throw. At the point of death, an unseen hand stopped him, and he heard a voice: "My beautiful devotee, I appreciate your vow and your one-pointed devotion. You wanted to do something for My sake, and you are trying to do that at any cost—even at the cost of your life! I accept your worship and reveal Myself to you."

The story of Sakkiya proves that it doesn't matter in what way you approach God. Choose any way you want; just be one-pointed in your devotion. Then you will experience God-realization.

The Fox and the Lice

nce upon a time, there lived a fox. Some lice thought that the fox's fur would make a nice jungle for them to live in, and soon millions of lice were all over its body. It was a terrible thing. The fox rubbed and scratched and did everything, but it couldn't get rid of them.

One day, the fox went to a pond to have a drink of water. As it placed its front paws in the water and started to drink, it noticed that the paws in the pond were suddenly free of lice. The lice had crawled up the fox's body because of the water.

The fox is a very cunning animal. It thought, "Ah, here is the trick!" It found a small stick, took one end of it in its mouth, and then slowly walked into the water. All the lice began to move up the fox's legs to get away from the water. The farther into the water the fox went, the higher the lice climbed. When the water touched the fox's abdomen, the lice moved onto its back. Little by little, the fox went in deeper, until all the lice were crowded onto its head. It went deeper still, until only its nose and the stick were out of the water. The lice moved onto the stick; only a few stayed on the nose. Then the fox took a deep breath, held its breath, and submerged its whole body. The few remaining lice moved onto the stick. At that moment, the fox simply let go of the stick. The lice floated away, and the fox walked out of the pond totally free of botheration.

Spiritual practices are like nice sticks to get rid of all our "lice"—all our attachments and undesirable habits. They help to free us from all that binds us, so that we can attain liberation.

The Lion and the Sheep

nce a mother lion was running for her life from a hunter. She was fully pregnant at the time, and as she was running, the baby lion came. She knew that if she stopped to take care of the cub, they would both be killed, so she ran away.

Now the place where the cub was delivered was near a big flock of sheep. So, naturally, all the sheep came around. And when they saw the baby, they all took care of it. The lion cub started drinking milk from the mother sheep and grew up as a little lamb. It began to say, "Baa, baa, baa," because what else could it do? That's all it heard. Things went on this way for quite some time. The lion cub grew into a nice, big lion, but even though it had the body of a lion, it acted like a sheep.

One day, another lion came that way and began chasing the sheep. As the sheep were running, the hunter-lion noticed another lion running in the midst of the flock. So it ran fast, bit the back of the fleeing lion, and made it stop. "What is this nonsense? Why are *you* running?" it asked.

"Baa," was all the other lion said.

"Hey, fellow, don't you know who you are?"

"Baa."

The hunter-lion, embarrassed by this sheep-like behavior, caught the timid lion by the tuft and brought him to the stream. "Look there! See who you are and stop bleating!" And they both looked at their reflections in the water.

The bleating lion said, "I look like you!"

"Yes. You are a lion."

"Is that so?"

"Yes. Take a good look."

And as it was looking, its tail went up in the air. It stood up straight and immediately started roaring. Finally, the lion realized who it really was.

Enlightening Tales

Just like the timid lion in the story, we, too, have forgotten our true nature. We have been hypnotized, in a way, since birth to think of ourselves as limited beings. One day we will realize that we are nothing less than the image of God. That is what is called spiritual awakening.

The Demon and the Curly Hair

nce there was a man who wanted to accomplish extraordinary feats. So he went to the forest and approached a great yogi who knew all the different sound formulas, which we call mantras. He begged the yogi to give him a mantra that would enable him to control a demon. The demon would then obey him and do all that he asked. The yogi said, "I can do it, but I warn you: you must always give him work or he will devour you."

The man thought, "Oh, there is a lot to do in this world. I can find thousands of jobs for him." And he confidently replied, "Don't worry. Please give me the mantra."

So the yogi initiated him. The man then went to a secluded spot and started doing *japa* (repetition) of his new mantra. He repeated it more and more, until he had built up the vibration that would attract the demon. Finally, a huge demon appeared. It even frightened the man a little.

"Master," asked the demon, "why did you call me? Give me some work."

"All right. Build a huge palace and fill it with the finest furniture." He thought the demon would take some time to do all that, and that he, himself, would be able to sleep until the job was finished. He was very tired after doing all the *japa*. But, suddenly, the demon reappeared.

"Sir, the palace is ready. What now?"

"What? Already? Hmm. . . Well, what can I do with just a palace? I must have a hundred servants to look after it."

"Okay." He snapped his fingers. "Servants are on the job."

"What about some vehicles?"

Snap! "There, many beautiful cars are in the garage: Rolls Royces, Cadillacs, Thunderbirds—complete with drivers and tanks full of gas."

"Well, I'm hungry," the man said.

Snap! There were fine dishes on a table, as well as a few maids to

serve. The man was puzzled. "What is this? The moment I request anything, immediately it comes. It doesn't even take a second."

"Well, now what?" demanded the demon, "I can't be without work."

The man was confused as to what to say, because the demon didn't even allow him time to think. He tried his best to give the demon things to do, but everything got finished immediately.

Then the demon said, "If you don't give me work, I will eat you."

The man started running to find his guru, with the demon following close behind. He ran and fell at the yogi's feet. "Oh, please save me. I don't want this demon anymore. He does everything immediately, and I can't satisfy him."

"Child, I told you, but you didn't listen to me."

"Please, don't lecture me now. This is not the time for advice. The demon is at my back!"

"Okay, I'll take care of him; don't worry."

The yogi plucked one curly hair from his head and gave it to the demon. "Please straighten this hair and stand it on its end."

The demon held the bottom of the hair in one hand and slowly pulled the other hand up until it reached the top to straighten the hair; then he let go in order to have the hair stand on its end. But how can a curly hair stand on its end? Of course, it fell down. Again the demon tried, and again it fell down.

"Well, are you finished yet?" asked the yogi.

"No, I'm still trying," answered the demon.

The guru then turned to his student and said, "Whenever you want some work done, tell the demon to put aside the hair and do the work. Then, when he's finished with the work, he can go back to the hair. That way, the demon will always have something to do."

The mind can do anything and everything just like the demon—that's why it's so restless. So give it a curly hair. The curly hair is your japa. *Whenever the mind is not fully occupied with some work, let it repeat the mantra. That way, it will always be calm and under your control.*

The Power of Maya

evendra, the king of all the celestial beings, once became curious about maya, the power of illusion. So Narada, the celestial devotee of Lord Narayana, appeared before him. Narada travels everywhere, all over the cosmos, helping people. Devendra asked him: "Narada, please explain to me about the power of maya. How does it affect people? Does it delude everyone?"

Narada replied, "Well, it's not possible for me to tell you. But if you would like to experience it for yourself, I can help you to do that."

"Okay, let me experience that a little."

So Narada said, "All right. Just go down to the world like an ordinary person. Travel around. You will see everything and will have the opportunity to experience maya's clutches."

Thus it happened that Devendra came down to the earth, and as he was wandering through a small village, he saw a few piglets. They were crying, and he wondered why. He looked around and saw a dead pig lying there. He found out that it was the mother pig. She had died suddenly, and all the little ones didn't know what to do. They didn't even know that the mother was dead, so they still ran all over the body, trying to get some milk. They were very hungry, and because they couldn't get any milk, they were crying.

When Devendra saw this, immediately his heart overflowed with compassion. "Oh, poor piglets. I should do something to help them. How can I see this and just walk away? But the only one that can satisfy them is the mother. All right then, I'll leave my body and get into that of the mother pig."

When Devendra got into the mother pig's body, the pig got up as if it were just awakening from sleep. Immediately, all the piglets were so happy. They were running around and around getting plenty of milk. Seeing their joy, Devendra thought, "Until they grow, I'll remain here.

Because if I go now, they will have the same problem again."

So Devendra remained in the pig's body as the little ones slowly started growing up. Meanwhile, the mother pig met a nice male pig, and they became friendly; and after some time, they had another batch of piglets, and another batch, and still another. Every time, at least a dozen more piglets were born. The family started growing, and Devendra was so happy. "Oh, boy," he thought, "look at my children and grandchildren and great grandchildren."

Years rolled by. All the celestial beings were wondering, "What has happened to Devendra? Where is he?" So they started looking for him. When Narada came by, they ran to meet him and asked, "Narada, what has happened to our king? You told him to do something, and we haven't seen him since."

"Oh, do you want to see him?"

"Certainly. We are without a king, and we want him back."

"Okay, I'll show you where your king is. There he is," said Narada, as he pointed to the pig.

"How dare you point to a pig and say our king is there!"

"But that *is* your king."

"But he's just wallowing in the mud; he's dirty all over and eating all kinds of filthy things. That can't be our king!"

"Yes, that is Devendra."

"Then we should go and save him."

Without a moment's delay, they all went down and pleaded with him, "Devendra, please, what are you doing in this pig's body? Get out of it at once!"

But Devendra just made some contented pig grunts and replied, "Why are you bothering me? I am a big mama here, a great grandma. Look at my big family. I don't know who this Devendra is that you're talking about. I am super happy here. Do you think your Devendra is this happy?"

The celestial beings looked at Narada and asked, "Narada, what is this? Is there any way to get him free?"

"The only way is to get rid of his family—to kill the piglets. Maybe then he'll realize the truth. It may be a harsh thing to do, but if you want to save him, there's no other way."

"All right, they agreed." And so they started killing all the piglets, one after the other. Every time one died, the mother pig cried and cried and cried. But the celestial beings really wanted to get their king out of the pig's body, so they killed all the piglets. Then they killed the father pig. Ultimately, the mother pig was left alone, and the celestial beings asked, "Are you ready to come out now?"

"What do you mean, 'Come out'? I have to go find another guy and start a new family. Why did you kill my family? Who are you people? Get out of here!"

At this point, Narada said to the celestial beings, "You still have to do one more thing. Chop off her head."

So they chopped off the head of the mother pig. Then the spirit came out. As soon as he got released, Devendra looked around and said, "What am I doing here? Why are all these dead pigs around me? Why did you bring me here?"

Then the celestial beings explained, "Sir, you were in that body."

"Me—in that body?! How horrible! Come on; let's go. I don't even want to stand here and see all this."

Then Narada looked at him and smiled, "Now, Devendra, you know the power of maya."

The play of maya can easily deceive you. As long as you are caught in it, it appears to be heaven to you. That's why the greatest person is the one who knows his or her own true nature and is not blinded by the illusory pleasures of the world.

True Surrender

beautiful story in the ancient Hindu epic, the *Mahabharata*, clearly teaches what is meant by true surrender to God.

The Pandavas and the Kauravas were cousins in the royal family. After the father of the Pandavas died, all the children were raised together in one household. As they grew up, the Pandavas became known and loved by all for their virtue and valor, and this made their cousins jealous. The eldest of the Kauravas, Duryodhana, couldn't bear the growing wealth and renown of the Pandavas and decided on a plot to dishonor them.

He tricked the eldest Pandava, Yudhisthira, into playing a game of dice in which Yudhisthira lost all that he had, including his wife, the beautiful Queen Draupadi. In ancient times, when you wanted to show that you had won a victory over someone, you did something that would dishonor him. So Duryodhana decided to have Draupadi dragged into the court and stripped of her sari. By doing this, he would ruin the reputation of the Pandavas.

A sari is six or seven yards of material that is gracefully wrapped around the body and then tucked in with delicate folds. Duryodhana's brother began to pull Draupadi's sari, and though she was clutching it tightly, very soon he succeeded in pulling out one round, and then almost a second round of the sari. Draupadi was very frightened. She was calling out to God in the form of Lord Krishna.

"Krishna, Krishna!" she cried, but her cries went unanswered. In another minute, the entire sari would be pulled off. Her strength could never match her assailant's. Realizing the situation, she thought to herself, "This is the final round of my sari. If I lose this also, I will be disgraced." In that moment, a great realization dawned: "What am I doing? I cannot take care of myself anymore. Lord Krishna, if you want me to face this disgrace, I will accept it. I totally trust you; my life is in your hands." And with that,

she let go of the sari and held up her hands crying, "Krishna!"

Draupadi just stood there calling and crying to her beloved Lord, while Duryodhana's brother mercilessly pulled the last round of her sari. But as he pulled, the cloth kept coming. After the last round, there was another and another and still another. He pulled again and again, yet there seemed to be no end to the sari. He kept pulling and pulling and pulling. Yards and yards and yards of sari seemed to be coming from nowhere. Eventually, Duryodhana's brother became exhausted and could pull no more. Draupadi was saved!

Even God cannot come and help you as long as you feel you can take care of yourself. Complete surrender means to give up totally and to depend entirely on God.

The Puzzle

 businessman was having a meeting with his partners at home. His daughter, a very intelligent little girl, kept interrupting them with all sorts of questions. The man wanted to keep her occupied for a while so that he could continue with his meeting. He looked around for something to amuse her and noticed a map of the world in a magazine. He took the map, tore it into pieces, and gave it to her.

"Daughter," he said, "I know that you are studying geography. Here you have all the pieces of a map. Try to put the map back together."

Without any hesitation, she replied, "All right, Dad; I'll do it!"

The girl took the map, sat down in a corner, and began examining the pieces. She didn't really know much about geography, so she was just looking at the various lines with tiny names written here and there. It was very confusing. After a while, she happened to turn over one of the pieces and saw a small section of a nose. She turned over another piece and saw a finger. On the third piece was a toe. So she started turning over all the pieces and found that she was looking at different parts of the human body.

It was very easy for her to put together the human body, because she knew where the eyes, the nose, and the arms should go. So, she put them all together and then placed a sheet of cardboard on top and carefully turned it all over. On the other side was the picture of the world, all intact.

She rushed to her father, happily announcing, "Dad, it's all back together now."

Her father had never expected her to do the puzzle so quickly. He said, "Daughter, I thought that you knew very little geography. I gave you the puzzle because I just wanted you to have something to do for a while. How did you put it together so fast?"

His daughter said, "It was easy, Dad! Just turn it over and look at the other side."

So her father turned over the puzzle and saw the human figure.

His daughter beamed. "Now do you see, Dad? I just put the man together and, automatically, the whole world came together, too.

Set the individual right and you'll set the world right, too. The best way to bring true peace to the world is by first finding that peace within yourself and then sharing it with one and all.

The World Is Your Projection

ri Ramakrishna tells this beautiful story about the nature of the mind.

Several people were walking early in the morning when they saw a man lying by the side of the road. The first person who passed him said, "He must have spent the whole night in the gambling casinos and couldn't make it home, and he fell asleep along the way. Gamblers are always like that."

The next person to come by said, "Poor man, he must be really sick. Well, probably it's best not to disturb him." And he walked away.

The third person said, "Humph! You dirty fellow, you didn't know how much to drink. Someone probably gave you some free whiskey. You drank a lot, and now you can't even get up."

The last person said, "To a saint, nothing matters. Even if he is lying on the pavement, he'll just be communing with God. Well, probably, he is above this physical consciousness. Let me not disturb him." And he bowed to the man and walked away.

All four saw the same person, but each saw him differently, because each one projected something of himself.

The entire world is nothing but your own projection. It is based on your thoughts and mental attitude. If there is hell in your mind, you won't see heaven anywhere. If there is heaven in your mind, even hell will be a heaven for you.

God or Dog?

nce there was a man who prayed to God every day in this way, "O God, I really want You to come in person to have a nice sumptuous lunch with me." Because he was continually asking for this, God appeared one day and said, "Okay, I'll come."

"God, I'm so happy," said the man. "When can You come? You must give me some time to prepare everything."

"Okay," said God, "I'll come on Friday."

Before God left, the man asked, "May I invite my friends?"

"Sure," God said. Then He disappeared.

The man was so excited. He invited everybody he could think of, saying, "God, Himself, is coming to *my* house for dinner!" And he began making preparations for all kinds of delicious dishes.

By noon on Friday, everything was ready. A huge, specially decorated dining table was set up. There was a beautiful garland of fragrant flowers and rosewater to wash God's feet when He arrived. All the man's friends were there. The man knew that God was always punctual, so when the clock started chiming twelve, he said, "Hmm. I wonder what has happened? God can't be late. He wouldn't disappoint me. Human beings may be late, but not God."

He was puzzled, but decided to wait another half-hour to be sure that God wasn't coming. Still, God didn't appear. The guests began sneering, "You fool! You said God was coming. We had our doubts all along: why on earth would God come to eat with you? Let's go!"

The man cried, "No. Please wait just a few more minutes!" But as he stepped into the dining room to check one more time, to his dismay, he saw a huge black dog right up on the elegant dining table, ravenously eating everything in sight.

"Oh, no!" cried the man. "God knew that this dog had come to defile

the food. That's why He didn't want to eat it." He grabbed a big club and started beating the dog furiously. The dog whimpered and ran away.

"Well, what can I do now?" the man asked his guests. "Now, neither God nor you can eat the food because it has been polluted by a dog. I know that's why God didn't come."

Slowly, everyone left. The man felt so bad that he went into his shrine room and started praying. After some time, he heard a soft moaning sound. He opened his eyes and saw God there before him. But God was covered all over with slings and bandages. Bruises and abrasions blotched His face.

"Oh, dear! What happened?" asked the man. "You must have been in a terrible accident."

"It was no accident," said God, "it was you!"

"Why do You say it was me?"

"Because I came punctually at noon and started eating all the delicious food. Then you came and beat me. You clubbed me and broke my bones."

"But You didn't come!"

"Are you sure *nobody* was eating your food?"

"Well, yes, there was a horrible, big black dog. He was right up on the table devouring everything. I beat him and chased him away. I was sure You didn't come because You knew about the dog."

"Who do you think that dog was, if not Me? I really wanted to enjoy your food. Who can better appreciate food and eat plenty of it than a dog? So I decided to come in the form of a dog."

At last the man understood. He fell to the floor and begged God for forgiveness.

Everything is God. Don't look for God only in heaven or on the altar. See God in all of creation and serve Him in all of the forms around you.

When Will You See God?

 young man went to the great saint Sri Ramakrishna and said, "Sir, I want to see God right away!"

Sri Ramakrishna said, "Before you see God, we will go to bathe in the Ganges." He took the young man to the Ganges and told him, "All right, dip." But as the fellow dipped, Sri Ramakrishna held him under the water. Immediately, the devotee started fighting for breath. When he knew the young man could not stay under any longer, Sri Ramakrishna let him up.

As the young man stood gasping on the riverbank, Sri Ramakrishna asked him, "What were you thinking about while you were under the water? Were you thinking of your money, your wife, your son, your name, your fame, your profession?"

"All I could think about was getting some air!"

"Good! When you have that kind of yearning for God, you will see Him right away."

In order to realize God, you need total, one-pointed yearning. So if you are not seeing God, know that the mind is still wanting other things.

King Janaka's Enlightenment

he scriptures say that real enlightenment can happen in the time it would take for a good horseman, who already has one foot in the stirrup, to mount his horse. In a fraction of a second, you can experience the Truth. King Janaka wanted to get that kind of enlightenment, so he invited all the sages and saints, all the learned people who could help him have that experience, to come to his court. Many great people came and quoted all the scriptures, but still Janaka didn't get the experience he was seeking.

One day, a saint by the name of Ashtavakra came to the area. He had been a saint even before he was born. It's true. While he was still in his mother's womb, he heard his father performing all kinds of prayers and rituals, but with a lot of mistakes. The child couldn't help laughing. The father looked around and wondered, "Who could be laughing at me?" Then he realized that it was the little fellow inside the womb. "You devil," he said, "you haven't even come out yet and already you have started to criticize me! What's wrong with what I'm doing?"

Ashtavakra answered from inside the womb, "Dad, you are not reciting properly; you are making so many mistakes."

"My goodness," said the father, "even now you are putting me to shame. What will happen when you come out?" Even though he was a great person, in a fit of anger, the father cursed his son with these words: "When you come out, everybody is going to laugh at *you*. Your body is going to be as crooked as possible—it's going to be bent in eight ways. Every time you take a step, your body will shake all over." And that's how he came to be known as Ashtavakra, which means "eight bends."

So Ashtavakra heard of King Janaka's situation and went to the palace. When he tried to enter, the gatekeepers just laughed at him, saying, "What are *you* going to do in there?" They doubted his capacity because of his strange-looking body.

"But I must see the king; I've come to help him," said Ashtavakra.

Again they laughed at him. Ashtavakra looked at them with pity and said, "Well, probably that's why you're out here and not sitting inside. Poor fellows." When Ashtavakra looked at them that way, they got frightened. They stepped aside, and he just walked in.

Unfortunately, as he approached the king, everybody in the court started laughing, too. Ashtavakra just ignored them, coming straight to the point. "Maharaj," he said, "I heard that you have a problem."

Immediately, Janaka recognized him. He got off the throne, received Ashtavakra with all respect, and saw to it that he was comfortably seated. "Yes, sir," he replied, "this is my doubt: the scriptures say that the supreme wisdom can be imparted within a fraction of a second. I really want to experience that, but no one seems to be able to do that for me."

"Ah! Do you *really* want to experience that?"

"Yes, I do."

"Okay, I can certainly do it; but it should be just between you and me. I don't think these butchers can understand anything. Ask them to leave the hall."

Calling someone a "butcher" was a big insult, so the people assembled in the court immediately became angry. "How dare he call us butchers!" they exclaimed.

But Ashtavakra coolly responded, "Don't be angry; I'm only telling the truth." The others demanded an explanation for such an insult, and Ashtavakra asked them: "What is the nature of a butcher? If you bring him a goat, what will he look for in the goat? Will he look for the soul? No. His interest is only in the physical features and the weight of the goat. The butcher is not interested in the spirit of the goat. What is it that you people did when I walked in? What is it that you saw that made you laugh?"

When he said this, they understood their mistake. "Yes, we saw only the body."

"So, you didn't see me; you saw the body. The body consists of flesh and bones. You were interested only in flesh and bones; so what is the difference, then, between you and the butcher? You can just leave; you are not fit for anything." So they left the court feeling very ashamed.

Then Ashtavakra asked Janaka to tell him what he had read. Janaka

said, "The scriptures say that if I am a good rider, and if I stand with one foot in the stirrup, by the time I throw the other leg across the horse, I should get enlightened."

"All right," said Ashtavakra, "we will follow the scripture exactly. Come on, bring a horse. Good. Now, stand like that. Are you ready?"

"Yes, I'm all set," said Janaka.

"Good. Now, did you read the verse before that one in the scripture? What was the previous verse?"

"The previous verse said that when you hear the utterance, the instruction, you get enlightened."

"And what was the qualification given for hearing the instruction?"

"The scripture said *sannyastam,* or renunciation. By renouncing everything, you become fit to hear the Truth."

"Ah, so you read that. Okay, having read that, are you ready? Have you renounced everything?"

"Oh," said Janaka, "I'm sorry; I haven't done that."

"Then how can you get enlightened? You must renounce everything that you would call yours. Or, in other words, remove yourself from all these identifications: 'I am the king,' 'I am a man,' 'I am this,' 'I am that.' Separate yourself from all this. You can give it all to me. It will be your offering to the guru. Just give them all, one by one."

"Okay," agreed Janaka. "I am giving my kingdom to you. I am giving my body. I am giving my intelligence. I am giving my ego."

Then Ashtavakra asked, "Are you ready to listen to the Truth?" But there was no answer. He couldn't even hear what the teacher was saying. Janaka just stood there without even saying, "Yes, sir." Actually, even to say *"he* stood there" is wrong. The body stood there. He had completely removed himself from all these identifications. He became the pure "I," that's all.

So, at that point, Ashtavakra said, "Okay, now I know that you have given up everything. You are just the pure 'I.' But unfortunately, as the pure 'I,' you are fit for nothing. The spirit needs a body, a mind, and an intellect in order to function. Even to hear me you need to have a little ego and the sense of hearing; so I give that back to you. But remember, you gave everything to me, and I am giving it back to you. It's not yours; I'm simply lending it to you. Now, make use of your body and mind and jump onto the horse." And as he was jumping, Ashtavakra said, "Thou art That! You are that Supreme Bliss! You are that Supreme Peace! You are that *Brahman!*" And in an instant, King Janaka realized the Truth.

The worldly "I" should renounce everything and become the pure "I"; instead of identifying with the body and mind, it should isolate itself. Once you do that, you will realize the Truth. Then, while remaining established in the Truth, you can use the body and mind in the service of humanity.

Who Am I?

here is a story from the *Upanishads* that tells about the king of the gods, Indra, and the king of the demons. In the story, Indra represents the refined, more spiritually evolved individual, while the king of the demons represents someone who has not yet purified himself. It goes like this:

Once the king of the gods, Indra, and the king of the demons went to the same teacher. They both asked the same question: "Master, please tell me who I am."

The teacher gave the same answer to both. He said, "Go to the well, look down, and see what is reflected in the water."

So they both went to the well, looked, and each saw his own physical reflection. Immediately, they both said, "That is me!" and went home.

The king of the demons started decorating, adoring, and indulging his body in every way. He ate well, slept well, and allowed all the senses to enjoy whatever they wanted. Indra, however, began to question: "How could *I* be that? Yes, I saw the reflection of my body, but I have read in the scriptures that the 'I' never changes. It is eternal, ever clean, ever pure. It is never born, never dies. But a body is born, it dies, and in between it changes every minute. How could that be the Self? I think I made a mistake. I did not understand him correctly. Let me go back and ask him."

By this time, several years had gone by. Indra went to the Master again. The Master said, "Who is asking this question now?"

"Well, the mind," Indra replied.

"Then, that is you. Now go!"

Indra went home. Again he started thinking and thinking and thinking. Twelve years or so went by. He analyzed: "I don't see how *I* can be the mind either. It often gets very crazy. It's not always the same. It fluctuates, gets excited, gets depressed. It forgets. There are lots of changes in the mind. That cannot be the Self. I think I should go back to the teacher again."

Enlightening Tales

This time, the Master said, "Who is watching the mind going through all these changes? *That* is the Self."

Indra went back, contemplated, and realized, "Yes, *That* never changes. *That* is always the witness of everything. *That* is who I am."

The Self is the eternal, never-changing One. Anything that changes, such as the body and mind, can never be the Self. Once we realize our true Self, we will see the same Self everywhere and experience the Oneness.

Let the Sun Shine In

here once was a little girl who didn't want to be in the sun, so she said, "Go away, sun, I don't want you!" She went inside, closed all the doors and windows, sat in the darkness, and started cursing the sun: "I don't want to see you anymore! Don't you *dare* come into my house!"

After a while, the little girl slowly opened the door, but the sun started pushing in. The girl shouted, "No! Get out!" and slammed the door in the face of the sun. A little while later, she started to open the door again, and again the sun came in.

The girl cried, "What is this? Aren't you ashamed? Don't you have any pride? I am scolding you. Aren't you offended? Why don't you stay away? Why do you want to come into my house?"

The sun just smiled and said: "That's my nature. If anybody opens the door, I just walk in. I don't wait for your invitation, and I am not offended by your scolding. All I need is an open door. If the door is open, even if you don't want me, you can't stop me from coming in."

God is like the sun, shining on everyone equally. And just like the sun, God is always there outside the door of your heart. If you open that door, even a little bit, God will come shining in.

The Poor Man's Karma

nce upon a time, there was a very, very poor man. Because of his poverty, he began to appeal to God. He would say, "O Lord Siva! O Mother Parvati! Please help me!" And he got into the habit of repeating the names of Siva and Parvati.

One day, he was walking on the road. Just at that moment, Lord Siva and Mother Parvati were also going for a walk, and they heard him. They saw him tottering down the road looking very weak. So, as a mother, Parvati felt compassionate and asked Lord Siva, "Don't you see him? He is one of our sons. I think he has suffered so much. We should probably give him some help."

Siva replied, "Why are you asking me? You are the Mother of the whole universe. Why don't you do something yourself?"

"But I want to know how you feel; shall we do something for him?"

"Well," said Lord Siva, "he is purging his karma by this suffering. He had a lot of money in his previous birth, but he never spent even a dollar for charity. He never helped any poor people. He never helped anyone who really wanted to lead a good life. He spent all his money on gambling and drinking, and on all kinds of luxuries and sensual enjoyments. He exploited many people and committed many crimes. He made many people suffer. So, naturally, he is poor now. He has to undergo this suffering; what can I do? It is his destiny. He's not ready to receive our help now. When the right time comes, he will certainly receive help."

"Oh, but I feel he has suffered enough," said Parvati. "Don't you see that he is constantly calling on you and me? Can't you supersede the karma?"

"All right then," said Siva, "you go ahead and try."

Parvati was so happy. Immediately, she took a big bundle of gold coins and dropped it about a hundred feet down the road. "I don't want to give it to him directly," she said. "This way, he will just see it and think that

he has found a great treasure." They both watched to see how happy the poor man would be when he found the money.

All this time, the man was walking. Suddenly, a thought came: "I may be poor and suffering so much, but still am I not much better off than many other people? So many people have handicaps. A blind man would not even be able to walk like me. Let me try to imagine what it would be like to be blind. . ." So he picked up a stick, closed his eyes, and walked about a hundred and fifty feet, pretending to be blind. Then he dropped the stick and cried, "God, thank you for having given me eyes that can see. I accept my suffering. I'm much better off than a blind man." And he continued to walk down the road.

Parvati looked at Siva, and Siva looked at Parvati. "What do you say, Parvati?" Siva asked.

"Honey, you are right. Even if we want to give something, it's not enough; a person has to deserve it."

God is all-merciful; He is not here to punish us. If we go through suffering, it is due to our own karma. Unless and until we purge our karma, even if somebody wants to come and help us, we won't be able to receive it.

The Pilgrimage

 undreds and thousands of people were making a pilgrimage to a holy place. In those days, they couldn't drive or fly—everyone had to walk. Along the way, a gentleman was sitting and watching all the pilgrims. All of a sudden, he saw a strange-looking person walk by, sort of a crude, ugly fellow. He stopped the fellow and asked, "Hey, who are you? You don't seem to be a pilgrim."

"Sir, how can you see me? Nobody is supposed to be able to see me."

"That doesn't matter. The fact that I am asking means I am seeing you. So tell me, who are you?"

"I am the Messenger of Death."

"Where are you going?"

"I'm going to the holy place of pilgrimage."

"Oh, I see. Are you going to worship there?"

"No, sir, that's not my job. I am going there to do my job."

"What is your job?"

"God has sent me to take away some lives. Some people have been assigned to leave their bodies, and the pilgrimage will provide a good excuse for that. The sanitary conditions will not be that good, so people can easily fall sick."

"So, what is it that you are going to do?"

"Well, I'm going to create some cholera there."

"How many are you going to kill?"

"I've been assigned to take four hundred and fifty people."

"All right. If God said to do that, then you have to do it. Go ahead and do your job."

So, the strange-looking fellow continued on his way. After the holy festival was over, all the pilgrims returned along the same route. Again the gentleman was seated, watching the pilgrims as they passed by. He asked some of them, "How did everything go?"

"Everything went well," they replied, "but, unfortunately, cholera broke out and many, many people died."

"Is that so? How many people died?"

"Oh, about fifteen hundred."

"What?!"

"Yes, sir; fifteen hundred people died. Didn't you see the newspaper?"

"Well," he thought, "let me wait for the Messenger of Death, and see what he has to say." The gentleman was carefully watching and when he saw the strange-looking fellow coming, he called, "Hey, stop! Are you the same fellow I spoke to awhile back who was going to the holy place?"

"Yes, sir."

"What did you tell me?"

"That I was going to the pilgrimage to take some lives."

"How many lives did you say?"

"Four hundred and fifty."

"Do you know how many people died?"

"Yes, sir; I know that."

"How many?"

"Fifteen hundred."

"How could you do that? You were assigned to take only four hundred and fifty people."

"Sir, I only did my job. I killed only four hundred and fifty people."

"Then how did the rest of the people die?"

"They died out of fear. I am not responsible for that. They killed themselves."

Our worst enemy is fear. A person who lives with fear dies every minute. Be bold and say, "Whatever has to happen will happen; what's the use of being afraid of it?" Whatever comes, fear not.

The Horoscope

t was a joyous day for the king! After many, many years of wanting an heir, his wife at last gave birth to a baby. Immediately, the king called all the astrologers to predict the child's future. Many great astrologers came to study the boy's horoscope. Each one studied the charts. The signs were quite clear. "Sir," the astrologers said, "your son is not a good child. Because of him, you will die by the time he reaches the age of ten. In a way, he has come to kill you."

The king was furious. "You devils! You don't even know how to cast a horoscope. Throw them all in jail!"

One day, an astrologer from far away came to the kingdom. When the king learned of this, he immediately called for the astrologer and asked him to look at his son's chart. The astrologer studied the horoscope carefully and said, "I have never seen a horoscope like this! It's a very strong horoscope. Your son will live a long life and will be a great king. He will live for one hundred years after you have died." Now, this astrologer was a very clever man. He read the same chart as the others, but he presented the information in a completely different way.

The king was so happy. "Shower this man with gifts. He is a great astrologer. If there is anything you want, sir, just ask me."

"Well," the astrologer said, "I have just one request."

"Of course. What is it?"

"Please release those other poor astrologers from the prison. Their only crime was not being very smart. They know how to calculate, but they don't know how to communicate."

Mere education is not enough. You should know how to deal with people, how to communicate, how to live harmoniously with others. Then you will enjoy real peace and joy in life.

Bringing a Donkey to Market

nce upon a time, there lived an old man in a small village. He was a very poor man, but he had a donkey. One day he ran out of money, so he decided to sell the donkey. He called his young son and said, "Come, son, let's take the donkey to market so we can sell it and get some money."

"Okay, Dad," said the boy, "let's go."

They both set out for the market. After a while, the father saw that the boy was getting tired, so he said, "Son, you sit on the donkey. I'll walk alongside."

Soon they came to a small village. As they were passing through, all the village folks began to laugh. "Hey, look at that," they said. "That young, good-looking boy with so much energy is sitting on the donkey, while that poor, old, tottering man is walking. Why can't the young fellow walk and let the old man ride on the donkey?"

When they heard that, the boy said, "Dad, they're right. You should get up here, and I should get down." So that's what they did.

After a while, the father and son passed through another village. The villagers began to say, "My goodness, have you ever seen a father like that—allowing that poor little boy to walk while he sits on the donkey? What kind of hard-hearted father is he?"

The father and son looked at each other. Then the boy said, "Dad, I don't know what to do."

"Well, son, probably you should also come up on the donkey. We'll both ride on the donkey, and then the problem will be solved."

So they were both riding on the donkey when they came to the next village. "My goodness," said the villagers, "look at those two donkeys riding on the donkey. The poor, innocent animal can't even cry or express its suffering to anybody. Instead of the donkey carrying those two, they should carry the donkey."

"Son," said the father, "probably they are right. Let's try to do that." So they both got down, tied the donkey's hind legs with a rope, tied its forelegs with another rope, and then inserted a long pole. They each took hold of one end of the pole and continued to the marketplace carrying the donkey between them.

Just before entering the town, they had to pass over a small, narrow bridge. As they were crossing the bridge, a couple of wild donkeys suddenly came running by and bumped into their donkey. Their donkey got excited, tried to kick, and fell into the river.

The son looked at the father, and the father looked at the son. "Dad, what should we do now?" asked the boy.

"Well, son, let's go back home. There's no donkey to sell anymore. We should never have listened to all those people. We should have used our own common sense. We lost our donkey, and we didn't get any money, but at least we learned a good lesson."

It's not possible to please everyone. Instead, satisfy your own conscience by doing things without any selfish motive. Then you will be pleasing God.

The Secret of Happiness

 long, long time ago, God created the entire cosmos: the planets and the stars, the mountains and the rivers, and all the plants and animals; and the grand finale of the creation was the human being. After everything else was done, God called together all the co-workers who had helped with the creation and said: "Now we have created everything, but there is still one more thing to be done: I want everyone to be happy. I want to give them happiness—but I want them to have to look for it. All other things I have kept out in the open—they can easily see them and get them. But I want them to really search for happiness, so that when they find it, they will truly understand its value."

So all the co-workers thought and thought about where would be a good place to hide happiness. Finally, someone had an idea: "I've got it. Let's hide happiness at the bottom of the deepest ocean." But when they thought about it some more, they realized that, eventually, the human beings would learn how to go to the bottom of the sea, and then the challenge would be over.

Someone else suggested hiding it in outer space. But another co-worker said, "They will easily go even to the moon and Mars, so we can't hide happiness there either."

After much deliberation, they turned to God and said, "Sir, we can't think of a good place to hide happiness, because, eventually, the human beings will be able to reach everywhere."

Then, suddenly, one little co-worker jumped up and cried, "I've got it! The human beings will always be looking for happiness outside, through money, power, possessions, and achievements of all kinds. The best place to hide happiness is right in their own heart; it's the very last place they will ever think to look for it."

Everyone quickly agreed, "Oh, that's a great idea, really great!" And

God thought so, too—and that's why God hid happiness in the heart.

People who look for happiness all over may seem to be getting it for a while, but soon they are looking for it again. Such happiness is fleeting and mixed with a lot of troubles, worries, and disappointments. True happiness is not the product of doing something or getting something. It is within you as your essential nature. You are Happiness personified.

The Man Who Did Nothing

 king was once visiting one of the temples in his country. Almost all the temples were provided for by the king himself, so he just wanted to go and see if everything was being managed properly. He arrived at the time when the *prasad* (blessed food) was being distributed. Small cakes had been prepared and offered to God, and now they were being distributed to all the *sadhus* (spiritual seekers), the devotees, and the servants who worked in the temple.

The king was sitting and watching. Each person was given a cake. In the corner, there was a swami just sitting and doing nothing. He hadn't even attended the worship, but he, too, was given a cake. When the king saw that, he called out to the man distributing the food, "Who is that fellow? He doesn't seem to be doing anything. Why should he get *prasad?* He didn't even come to the *puja*. What does he do here?"

"Maharaj, he just sits there. We don't know what he does. We have never seen him doing anything."

"So, he does nothing?"

"It looks that way, sir."

"Let me find out," said the king, and he went to where the swami was sitting.

"*Sadhu!*"

"Yes?"

"Are you getting food here daily?"

"Yes, they are giving food to me."

"And what do you do for that?"

"Nothing."

"So you do nothing, and you get food?"

"That seems to be what's happening."

"Why should you be given food when you do nothing?"

"Well, Maharaj, it looks as though that is the most difficult job."

"Ah, is that so? Well, I can also do nothing."

"Okay, Maharaj, you can try."

So the king just sat there in front of the swami with his eyes closed for a few minutes and then he spoke: "See, I did nothing. You said it was the most difficult thing to do."

"Sir, please excuse me. You were not doing nothing. You were thinking of buying a few more horses for your stables."

Immediately, the king jumped up and fell at the *sadhu's* feet. "Yes, now I understand. Doing nothing doesn't mean simply sitting. The mind also should be totally still. I was doing something—not physically, but mentally. Now I realize what you mean by 'doing nothing.'" And the king called the man who distributed the *prasad* and told him, "In the future, see that he gets two cakes, not one."

The most difficult thing in life is not to do anything. When you realize that none of the things in the world, none of the people, none of the positions or accomplishments are going to make you happy, then you give up and surrender the ego. You feel, "I don't have to be doing anything or getting anything for myself." That is sannyas, *or renunciation. Then, all knowledge and wealth will come to you.*

The Last Straw

ou cannot say exactly what will open your mind to the Truth or when it will happen. Real knowledge or wisdom doesn't come little by little—it is instantaneous. When will it happen? Nobody can tell you; but even a small, ordinary thing could bring it about.

I will tell you a story about a saint named Patinatar. His father was a very rich man who had made a lot of money from shipping and other businesses. The father had seen many saints and sages and had studied extensively, but nothing had opened his mind to the Truth. He repeated his mantra regularly, faithfully performed the religious rituals, did all the spiritual practices, but wisdom had not dawned in him.

One day, he asked his son, Patinatar, to take his ship to go buy some merchandise. Patinatar went to an island and saw the poor people there. He spent all the money—millions of dollars—on helping those people. Patinatar realized that he couldn't go home with an empty ship, so he filled the entire ship with cow dung cakes, which are used as fuel. The dung cakes were probably worth a hundred dollars or less. Then he sailed home.

As soon as the boat arrived, some of the boatmen ran to the father and told him, "Your son has gone crazy. He spent all of your money, and all he came back with is cow dung." The father was so upset that he didn't even want to see his son. When Patinatar arrived at the house, his father was not even there to greet him.

Patinatar gave a small package to his mother and said, "Please give this to my father when he returns. I will see you later." With that, he walked out.

When the father came home, he asked, "Where is my son?" His wife told him that Patinatar had come and gone, and she gave her husband the package. When the father opened the package, he found a broken sewing needle and a note. The note said, "Even the eye of a broken needle will not

125

come with you on your final journey." As soon as he read those words, Patinatar's father immediately took off his fancy clothes, put on a loincloth, said good-bye to his house and his businesses, and walked out. Realization had dawned in him. He had heard many hundreds of religious stories before, he had read volumes, he knew all the philosophy, but nothing had opened his eyes until he saw those few words.

Realization can dawn with the smallest thing; it doesn't have to be a big blow. At any moment, anything could be the last straw for you. Then you are enlightened. Until then, you are still preparing yourself; you are getting ready for that moment.

Glossary

Ashram—a spiritual community where seekers practice and study under the guidance of a spiritual master

Bhagavad Gita—Hindu scripture in which Lord Krishna instructs his disciple Arjuna in the various aspects of Yoga

Brahman—the unmanifest Supreme Consciousness or Absolute God

Brahmin—Hindu priestly caste

Devendra—another name for Indra, the chief of the gods

Guru—(lit. remover of darkness); spiritual guide, teacher

Indra—king, lord or chief of the gods

Japa—concentrated repetition of a mantra or Holy Name

Karma—law of action and reaction

Karma Yoga—selfless service; work done without expectation of reward

Karma Yogi—one who does Karma Yoga

Krishna—incarnation of Lord Vishnu; teacher in *Bhagavad Gita*

Mahabharata—Hindu epic which contains the *Bhagavad Gita*

Maharaja—king

Mantra—(lit. that which makes the mind steady); a sound formula for meditation

Maya—illusory power of God

Narayana—Lord of the Universe; Lord Vishnu

Parvati—wife of Lord Siva

Pranayama—the practice of controlling the vital force, usually through control of the breath

Prasad—consecrated offering

Puja—worship service

Pujari—one who performs puja

Ramakrishna Paramahamsa, Sri (1836-1886)—saint of India, guru of Swami Vivekananda

Roti—an Indian bread

Rupee—basic unit of Indian currency

Sadhana—spiritual practice

Sadhu—spiritual seeker, often a wandering mendicant

Sannyas—renunciation

Sannyasi—member of the Holy Order of Sannyas; a Hindu monk

Sannyastam—to renounce

Sari—traditional dress worn by Hindu women

Satsanga—(lit. company of the wise); spiritual gathering or group

Siva—major Hindu deity; God as Auspiciousness

Swami or Swamiji—(lit. master of one's own self); lord; Hindu religious title usually for a sannyasi; a term of respect

Upanishads—the final portions of each of the *Vedas*, (the primary scriptures of Hinduism), which give the non-dualistic Vedanta philosophy

Vedanta—non-dualistic Hindu philosophy found in the *Vedas*

Vishnu—God as the Preserver; incarnated in various forms, such as Lord Rama and Lord Krishna

Yagna—sacrifice

Yoga—(lit. union); union of the individual with the Absolute; any course of endeavor that makes for such union; unruffled state of mind under all conditions

Yogi—one who practices Yoga